GREAT WAR LITERATURE

GCSE STUDY GUIDE

Written by W Lawrance

on

JOURNEY'S END

A PLAY BY R. C. SHERRIFF

Great War Literature GCSE Study Guide on Journey's End a Play by R C Sherriff
Written by W Lawrance

Published by:
Great War Literature Publishing LLP
Forum House, Stirling Road, Chichester PO19 7DN
Web site: www.greatwarliterature.co.uk
E-Mail: enquiries@greatwarliterature.co.uk

Produced in Great Britain

Design and production by Great War Literature Publishing LLP
Typeset in Neue Helvetica, ITC Berkeley Old Style and Trajan Pro

Great War Literature GCSE Study Guide on

Journey's End
a play by R. C. Sherriff

CONTENTS

PREFACE

Great War Literature Study Guides' primary purpose is to provide in-depth analysis of First World War literature for GCSE students.

There are plenty of other study guides available and while these make every effort to help with the analysis of war literature, they do so from a more general overview perspective.

Great War Literature Publishing have taken the positive decision to produce a more detailed and in-depth interpretation of selected works for students. We also actively promote the publication of our works in an electronic format via the Internet to give the broadest possible access.

Our publications can be used in isolation or in collaboration with other study guides. It is our aim to provide assistance with your understanding of First World War literature, not to provide the answers to specific questions. This approach provides the resources that allow the student the freedom to reach their own conclusions and express an independent viewpoint.

Great War Literature Study Guides can include elements such as biographical detail, historical significance, character assessment, synopsis of text, and analysis of poetry and themes.

The structure of Great War Literature Study Guides allows the reader to delve into a required section easily without the need to read from beginning to end. This is especially true of our e-Books.

The Great War Literature Study Guides have been thoroughly researched and are the result of over 30 years of experience of studying this particular genre.

Students must remember that studying literature is not about being right or wrong, it is entirely a matter of opinion. The secret to success is developing the ability to form these opinions and to deliver them succinctly and reinforce them with quotes and clear references from the text.

Great War Literature Study Guides help to extend your knowledge of First World War literature and offer clear definitions and guidance to enhance your studying. Our clear and simple layouts make the guides easy to access and understand.

INTRODUCTION

This play was originally performed in December 1928 and published the following year. The action takes place in a dugout, in a British trench near St Quentin in France. This is a story of the relationships between five officers between 18th and 21st March 1918, immediately prior to a major battle.

We experience everything from mundane discussions regarding the merits of pineapple over apricots, to the death of one of the officers and the impact this has on those left behind.

There are many moments of humour in the play, particularly at the beginning, which serve to intensify the horrors which the men are experiencing. By introducing humour and detailed personalities into the play, Sherriff demonstrates the human cost of the war which destroyed a generation of young men, the like of which would never be seen again.

JOURNEY'S END
A PLAY BY R. C. SHERRIFF

SYNOPSIS

ACT ONE

The play opens with Captain Hardy, alone in the dugout, trying to dry his sock, while singing a song to himself. Osborne arrives and the two men share a drink while Hardy finishes dressing. Hardy's regiment is being replaced at the front by Osborne's and the two men discuss what has been happening lately, and the likelihood of a German attack. They talk about the layout and condition of the dugout and trenches and Hardy hands over a list of supplies. The conversation turns to Stanhope - Osborne's company commander. Hardy appears critical of Stanhope's drinking, but Osborne defends him. Although Hardy should really wait and hand over to Stanhope personally, he chooses not to and leaves Osborne to pass on his messages.

The officers' servant - a soldier named Mason - appears and he and Osborne discuss that night's meal. Raleigh arrives: he is a new officer, fresh from England. Osborne welcomes him and, over a drink, it soon becomes clear that Raleigh already knows Stanhope. He explains that they had been at the same school, although Stanhope is three years older. Raleigh's devotion to his old school friend is obvious - in fact it would seem that Raleigh has used some of his family's influence to ensure that he would be assigned to Stanhope's Company. He reveals that Stanhope and his sister share a close friendship, a fact of which Osborne had not previously been aware. Osborne seems concerned that Raleigh might notice some changes in Stanhope and tries to prepare him, as well as explaining some of the routine of the dugout and the trenches.

Raleigh is introduced to Mason, who is worried because a tin which he thought contained pineapple chunks, turns out to be full of apricots and he knows that

Stanhope dislikes this particular fruit. Osborne tries to reassure him. Just then Stanhope arrives, together with Second Lieutenant Trotter. Stanhope is angry about the condition of the trenches and orders Mason to bring him some whisky. When he is introduced to Raleigh, Stanhope is shocked to see him and an uneasy atmosphere descends, which Osborne tries his best to cover up.

Raleigh is introduced to Trotter and the men sit down to eat, although Stanhope becomes angry once more when they discover that there is no pepper to go with their soup. While they eat, they discuss their position and their duties for that night. Raleigh is sent on duty with Trotter as it is his first time in the trenches. The man they have relieved - Hibbert - enters the dugout, declines any food and, complaining of a pain in his eye, goes straight to bed. Stanhope seems to think that Hibbert is faking his illness and is unsympathetic. Osborne turns the conversation to Raleigh and Stanhope expresses his surprise that of all the Companies in France, Raleigh should have been sent to his. He shows Osborne a photograph of Raleigh's sister and tells him how concerned he is at how much his personality has changed and how frightened he is.

Stanhope reveals his fear that Raleigh will write to his sister, Madge and reveal the truth about his drinking. Then he realises that he could censor Raleigh's letters and continue to keep his drinking a secret. By now Stanhope is quite drunk and very tired, so Osborne persuades him to sleep for a while, and then retires to bed himself.

ACT TWO

It is the following morning and Stanhope is on duty in the trench, while the other men are eating breakfast in the dugout. They talk about Stanhope, who they think looks unwell, although Raleigh seems embarrassed by the tone of the conversation and is reluctant to criticise his old friend. Sensing Raleigh's discomfort, Osborne changes the subject and they talk about the weather and gardening until Trotter goes to relieve Stanhope. Left by themselves for a short while, Osborne tells Raleigh that he used to play rugby for Harlequins and England, which impresses the younger man. They also discuss the war in general, although when Stanhope returns, Raleigh excuses himself and goes back to his own dugout to finish a letter.

Osborne and Stanhope talk over their immediate tasks, such as repairing the barbed wire, and also the anticipated German attack. Although it is only early in the morning, Stanhope starts drinking. He is very worried about Raleigh's letter and when he reappears with it, ready for posting, Stanhope tells him that he must leave it open on the table so that it can be censored. Raleigh is flustered and initially refuses to show his letter, saying that he will leave it until later. This fuels Stanhope's fears and he wrenches the letter from Raleigh's hand in a violent outburst. Raleigh is shocked by his friend's behaviour and quietly leaves the dugout to go on duty. Osborne is also stunned, but Stanhope turns on him too, before realising that his actions were unnecessarily harsh. He no longer wants to read the letter and throws it down on the table. Osborne offers to glance at it, just to set Stanhope's mind at rest and reads it quietly to himself. When he has finished, he offers to tell Stanhope what Raleigh has said and, although he dreads hearing it, Stanhope agrees. Osborne reads part of Raleigh's letter aloud, which reveals that he feels honoured to be serving with Stanhope; that Stanhope is always tired, but that this is because he is such a good officer who rarely sleeps and is always trying to cheer up the men, and also that the men love him. Raleigh is full of pride that Stanhope is *his* friend. Osborne sticks down the envelope and Stanhope stands, ashamed now that he had doubted Raleigh.

Later that day, Stanhope is issuing instructions to a Sergeant-Major when the Colonel arrives. The Sergeant-Major is excused and then the Colonel reveals that he wants Stanhope to organise a raiding party to be sent across No Man's Land to capture one or two enemy soldiers, in the hope of discovering the strength of the opposition. The Colonel suggests that Osborne should lead the raid and be supported by Raleigh. Stanhope tries to convince the Colonel that Raleigh is too inexperienced, but eventually it is agreed that there is no-one else who could go and the Colonel leaves.

Hibbert appears, having been asleep. He says he feels too unwell to remain at the front. Stanhope tells him that he is suffering from the same complaint himself, but Hibbert persists, saying that he wants to leave the front line and go for medical assistance. Stanhope stops him and says that he will not be allowed to leave: he is not that unwell. Hibbert becomes hysterical and goes to collect his belongings, saying that he is going to leave anyway. Stanhope fetches his revolver and, when Hibbert returns and tries to leave the dugout, a heated argument follows during which Hibbert tries to hit Stanhope, who becomes angry and tells Hibbert that, rather than allow him to leave, he would shoot him and make it look like an accident. Hibbert tells him to go ahead - he would rather be shot than have to spend one more moment in the trenches. The two men face each other and eventually, Stanhope replaces his revolver and speaks quietly to Hibbert, telling him how frightened he is. He appeals to Hibbert not to let his comrades down and somehow persuades him to stay, offering to go on duty with him to help calm his nerves.

Osborne comes into the dugout and Stanhope tells him that he is to lead the raid. Stanhope leaves to make arrangements with the Sergeant-Major and a sleepy Trotter appears from his bed. Osborne tells him about the raid and they agree not to discuss the details in front of Raleigh in case he becomes frightened. Osborne is reading *Alice's Adventures in Wonderland* and Trotter seems surprised by his choice of book, although he has never read it himself.

Stanhope returns and collects Hibbert, taking him out into the trench. Osborne and Trotter settle down to some letter writing and Raleigh comes off duty, having been relieved by Stanhope and Hibbert. He has been told about the raid, and is very excited, viewing it as an adventurous opportunity.

Colin Keith-Johnston as Captain Stanhope in Journey's End
at the Henry Miller Theatre, New York, March 22, 1929.
Photograph courtesy of NYPL Digital Gallery. Digital ID: 499286

ACT THREE

It is the following afternoon and Stanhope is nervously pacing the floor of the dugout, when the Colonel arrives. The two men discuss the plans for the raid. When Osborne and Raleigh come in, the Colonel offers them words of encouragement. Once Osborne and Stanhope are alone, Osborne asks Stanhope to take care of his personal effects, just in case he does not come back from the raid. Stanhope says he will do this, but refuses to acknowledge that Osborne might not return. Finally, Raleigh and Osborne are alone and they go over what will happen during the raid. Then they try to talk about anything else *except* the raid, until eventually the time comes for them to leave. Raleigh suddenly seems nervous, but Osborne calms him down. They leave the dugout, which remains empty, although the noise of the raid can be heard.

When all has gone quiet, Stanhope and the Colonel come into the dugout from the trench. The raid has resulted in the capture of one German soldier who is brought down into the dugout. Stanhope goes back out to talk to the men, while the Colonel interrogates the prisoner. Stanhope returns and the Colonel absent-mindedly asks whether all the men have returned safely, to which Stanhope replies, bitterly, that Osborne and six others have been killed. Raleigh enters the dugout and, after congratulating him, the Colonel leaves. Raleigh sits, dumfounded and in shock, on Osborne's bed. Stanhope has no words of consolation, but simply asks why he must sit there, rather than somewhere else.

Later that evening, Trotter, Stanhope and Hibbert, having dined, sit and tell stories and jokes. This has been a special dinner including chicken and champagne, but Raleigh has chosen to remain on duty in the trench, rather than join them. Hibbert reveals that Raleigh did not want to come to the dinner and preferred to be with the men. This news shakes Stanhope, who becomes angry and orders Hibbert to go to bed. Once they are alone, Stanhope tells Trotter that he is now second-in-command. Trotter promises not to disappoint Stanhope, and goes out to relieve Raleigh.

When Raleigh enters, Stanhope is angry with him for not attending the dinner and Raleigh makes matters worse by admitting that he has eaten with the men. Stanhope's temper becomes almost uncontrollable and Raleigh is confused, not just by Stanhope's attitude, but also about why they all had a celebratory meal when Osborne had just been killed. Stanhope angrily explains that the drinking and celebration are done to forget, not because he does not care. He dismisses Raleigh.

Very early the next morning, the officers wake up and prepare for the expected attack. Mason is told that he will have to join his platoon in the trench once he has completed his chores. The Sergeant-Major comes down to the dugout to get his instructions. Trotter comes out and calls for Raleigh and Hibbert to join him, before going out into the trench. Raleigh appears and pauses to say goodbye to Stanhope, who barely acknowledges him. Hibbert still has not appeared, so Stanhope calls him again, but when he does come out, he is reluctant to go into the trench. Eventually, Stanhope finds a way around the situation by asking Hibbert to accompany Mason into the trenches. Hibbert can hardly refuse this order and the two men leave. Various messages come down for Stanhope and he gets ready to go up himself. The Sergeant-Major comes down to tell him that Raleigh has been wounded. Stanhope tells him to bring Raleigh down to the dugout and, despite his surprise, the Sergeant-Major obeys and carries Raleigh to Osborne's bed. Raleigh has been badly wounded and Stanhope bathes his head. The two men talk briefly, although Raleigh does not understand the extent of his injuries. Stanhope conceals the truth from him and reassures him that he will be fine. Their friendship is restored as Stanhope briefly takes care of Raleigh in the few minutes before he dies.

A soldier comes down into the dugout and says that Trotter has asked for Stanhope to come up immediately. Stanhope pauses to touch Raleigh's head, before going up into the trench. Just as he does, a shell bursts just outside and the entrance caves in, extinguishing the one remaining candle. All is in darkness and the only sound is of the shells and machine-gun fire.

GLOSSARY OF TERMS

Some of the military language and terminology used in Journey's End can be confusing. We have included below a list of some of the terms or phrases from the play which may require explanation, in alphabetical order.

Billets - Lodging for a soldier, normally in a private home, farm outhouses or public buildings.

Boche - French slang for a German, also adopted by the British.

Dugout - A shelter dug underground. In the First World War, officers at the front essentially lived in these constructions which were sometimes joined together by a series of tunnels.

Funk - Fear or terror.

Lanyard - A cord worn around the waist or neck to secure a gun, knife or whistle.

Lewis Gun - A type of machine gun, used by the British during the First World War.

Log-book - The official record of what has taken place in a particular sector.

MC - Abbreviation for Military Cross. Established in December 1914, this medal was awarded for gallantry to officers, up to the rank of Captain, although it has since been expanded to include other ranks.

Minnies - A German trench mortar, actually named a 'Minenwerfer' which literally translates as 'mine-launcher'.

No Man's Land - Area of land between the front line trenches.

Parapet - The part of the trench which faces No Man's Land, raised to protect the men from enemy fire.

Pavé - French for a type of pavement, usually made of square cobbles on older roads.

Quartermaster-Sergeant - A senior non-commissioned officer who is responsible for supplies.

Sap - A communication trench dug at an angle from the main trench system.

Sentry Post - Position where a man could be positioned to stand guard or observe enemy activity.

Toch-emmas - Army slang for a trench mortar.

Trench Fever - A disease which was quite common in the First World War, causing high fever, headache an back or leg pain. It was transmitted by the lice that infested the men's clothing.

Very Lights - A flare fired from a gun.

Whizzbangs - Slang name used by the British for German artillery. Refers to the noise made by the travelling shell, followed by the explosion.

Wipers - Slang for the Belgian town of Ypres, which saw intense fighting throughout the First World War.

CHARACTERS

STANHOPE

General Description

The son of a country vicar, this young captain is the commanding officer of the company of men with whom Journey's End is concerned. Aged approximately twenty-one years, Stanhope has been in the trenches for almost three years, having gone into the army at eighteen. Physically, he is described as tall, thin, and having broad shoulders. The impression created is that he is fastidious about his appearance, having neatly brushed dark hair and a well-cared-for uniform. The description given of Stanhope also refers to the effects of serving in France for three years: although tanned, his face is pale and he appears very tired and drawn.

Character Analysis

Even before his first appearance, the conversation between Osborne and Hardy has already made it clear that Stanhope drinks heavily and through the course of the play, we learn that this is done to calm his nerves, which even he appreciates, are shattered. The alcohol also helps him to forget the horrors of everyday trench life and death. This early conversation tells us much more about Stanhope; for example he is fussy about the cleanliness of the trenches. Stanhope likes the trenches and dugouts to be well maintained and with good reason: ammunition stored improperly in wet or damp trenches can go rusty and malfunction; disease can easily be spread amongst the men due to poor sanitation; and he resents the idea that his men, who already have sufficient tasks to keep them occupied, should have to spend their time clearing up someone else's mess. To Stanhope, such inefficiency is intolerable. During this same conversation we also discover the high regard in which Stanhope is held. Osborne comments to Hardy that he does not know of anyone who is as good a commander as Stanhope and we learn how much Osborne loves him. Stanhope

This new edition of the Great War Literature GCSE Study Guide on Journey's End provides several new chapters and more detail and has been produced in response to requests and suggestions received from schools and examining boards, giving you the most valuable resource available.

is obviously an excellent officer, and has been awarded the MC (Military Cross - awarded to officers for bravery), so his courage is not in doubt to anyone except himself. He is concerned with the welfare of his men: but this concern, together with his experiences and fears have taken their toll on him both physically and mentally. He is a man on the verge of breaking down.

Stanhope appreciates that the war has changed him as a man. When his old friend Raleigh appears in his Company, Stanhope is shocked and he finds it difficult to disguise this. Ever since they were at school together Stanhope has always regarded it as his responsibility to look after Raleigh, particularly as their fathers were old friends. Now his task is harder than ever - taking care of a younger boy at school, and living up to his high expectations is completely different from looking after a junior officer in the front line trenches. He is also aware that Raleigh has always hero-worshiped him, and he is afraid of losing Raleigh's respect once it becomes clear how drastically different he has become. Stanhope would prefer it if Raleigh had been able to remember him as a boy-hood hero, rather than a broken man, which is how he now perceives himself. In addition he is also concerned that in writing home, Raleigh will betray Stanhope's altered nature and that this might not only shatter his image within his own family, but also with Raleigh's sister Madge, who he obviously loves and with whom he has an understanding. He is keen that Raleigh's sister should be proud of him, and never know of the ways in the which the war has changed him. His outburst when Raleigh refuses to hand over his letter is extreme and shocks his young friend, as well as Osborne, who has clearly never seen Stanhope behave in this way. However, Stanhope soon realises that he has behaved badly and his reaction to the content of Raleigh's letter shows how ashamed he is of his own shortcomings.

Stanhope is conscious of the impression he creates with his men and junior officers and the only person allowed to see him with his guard down is Osborne. Stanhope is very critical of himself but his opinion of his own shortcomings is not reflected by the men in his own Company, who, despite his obvious problems, continue to look up to and respect him. This is not a universally-held opinion, as we have already learned from Hardy that some of the men from outside his Company regard Stanhope's behaviour as somewhat freakish or laughable, especially when he is drunk. This may be, however, because it is easier for them to laugh at him than to appreciate that what has happened to him could just as easily happen to them.

Stanhope is a man with a strong sense of duty: while discussing plans with the Sergeant-Major, he suggests that, rather than retreat in the face of the enemy, the

Company will continue to go forward until they have won the war! This is said half-humourously: Stanhope obviously has no intention of retreating - it would be contrary to his orders - but also he wants to reassure the Sergeant-Major who seems to be worried about the strength of the anticipated attack.

Hibbert's supposed illness demonstrates another side of Stanhope who makes it clear that he will do whatever it takes for the good of his Company. This becomes clear in the episode where Hibbert attempts to evade further participation in the forthcoming attack. Stanhope initially threatens to shoot Hibbert - a fate which would have befallen him anyway, had he deserted. Then, when Hibbert breaks down, Stanhope tells him that he is experiencing exactly the same fears himself. In threatening to shoot Hibbert, we learn that Stanhope places the morale and well-being of the whole company above that of any one man, including himself. If Hibbert had been allowed to carry on behaving as he was, his duties would have suffered and the men might be put at risk as a consequence - a chance which Stanhope is not prepared to take. Stanhope is also aware that, by leaving, Hibbert would be placing an unfair burden on the officers left behind. He also knows that in the long run, it will be better for Hibbert to stay and face the enemy than run and never know if his courage would have failed him at the vital moment. Stanhope reveals his own fears to Hibbert both as a means of shaming the junior officer into staying and also to make him realise that feeling terrified is quite common and is nothing of which to be ashamed. This is an interesting point to note as earlier on, he had been worried that Raleigh's letter home might reveal his own fears and perceived weaknesses. Stanhope, it would seem, is more tolerant and forgiving of other people's defects than of his own. It is also worth noting that Stanhope never reveals Hibbert's actions to anyone, which demonstrates his loyalty to his men.

The news of the planned raid hits Stanhope hard. Initially he offers to take part himself, and then tries to persuade the Colonel that Raleigh is unsuited to the task, which shows that he still feels responsible for his old schoolfriend. Neither of these strategies work, as the Colonel cannot spare Stanhope, and there really is no-one else who can accompany Osborne. He is clearly worried at having to send anyone on this mission, which he feels is not worth risking the lives of his men. When Stanhope and Osborne part, there is an intensity of feeling between them, which is shown in the glances and awkward pauses in their conversation. Stanhope agrees to take care of Osborne's belongings but will not acknowledge the possibility that his friend might not return from the raid. He quite rightly points out that he would be lost without Osborne.

When Osborne is killed, Stanhope is bitter and angry and these are feelings which he takes out on Raleigh, who has returned safely. He acknowledges to Raleigh that in losing Osborne, he has lost his best friend and the one person in whom he could confide - he is unsure of how he will be able to continue without his "Uncle" by his side. He attempts to mask his emotions once again, by drinking and laughing with Trotter and Hibbert, but eventually reveals his true feelings in an angry outburst against Raleigh.

When his old schoolfriend is injured Stanhope reverts to his real personality, trying to spare Raleigh the knowledge of his impending death. This is the genuine Stanhope, as he was before he became damaged by his experiences in the war. He tenderly cares for Raleigh and looks after him to the very end. His status as hero is restored - both to Raleigh, to himself and to the audience: he has done his duty.

Portrayal and Development of Stanhope

As the central character in the play, the successful depiction of Stanhope was of vital importance to the play. In creating this character, Sherriff had looked to generate someone whom others would look up to, making him a leader and a hero, worth of Raleigh's worship. However, Sherriff also wanted to show the audience that the war could wreak havoc on any man - even one as seemingly gallant and respectable as Stanhope.

Sherriff takes Stanhope on a journey through the play. We know from Osborne that he is well liked and respected, but when Raleigh arrives, we see Stanhope's facade begin to crumble to a point where even Osborne questions his actions. Throughout the play, to demonstrate the changes in Stanhope's personality to both the characters and the audience, Sherriff presents him with a series of problems and issues. These include Hibbert's refusal to fight, the awful decision that Raleigh must take part in the raid and Osborne's death. Then, Sherriff shows us that, despite his own personal despair, Stanhope will always rise above his surroundings and circumstances to do the right thing.

Sherriff needed the audience to understand the depth to which Stanhope had fallen by depicting Raleigh's recollections of him as a schoolboy, so that the audience can appreciate the changes in his personality. In this way, Sherriff is able to show the path which Stanhope has taken - from the innocent sporting heroic boy of school days, to the broken, confused and ultimately still courageous young man at his Journey's End.

RALEIGH

General Description

Raleigh is the innocent young recruit who arrives, excited at being involved in the war, and particularly at being able to serve under his old schoolboy hero, Stanhope. He is described as a handsome, healthy, but somewhat naive and inexperienced young man.

Character Analysis

Upon first arriving, Raleigh is nervous and eager to please, although unsure of how he is supposed to behave. He talks enthusiastically to Osborne of his pre-war friendship with "Dennis" Stanhope. He reveals that he has used his uncle, General Raleigh's, influence to achieve this posting, because he desperately wanted to serve under his old schoolfriend. This is probably partly because Stanhope has always taken care of him and Raleigh hopes this will continue at the front, but also because he simply worships Stanhope and desperately wants to be with him.

Despite Osborne's friendly warnings about the effect that three years' fighting has had on Stanhope, Raleigh is still surprised by Stanhope's appearance and his less than enthusiastic welcome. It is as though Raleigh had expected their relationship to be exactly the same as it was when they were at school. Upon first witnessing Stanhope's drunkenness, Raleigh appears shocked and seems to prefer not to be in company with his old friend.

Stanhope's reaction to his letter also comes as a blow to Raleigh. He had not anticipated that his letter would need to be censored, presumably because he feels that Stanhope should trust him and he is embarrassed by the prospect of Stanhope reading the contents of his letter. Stanhope misreads Raleigh's reluctance and reacts violently towards him. Raleigh begins to understand the effects of the war on Stanhope, but is still confused, and disappointed by his friend's reaction. In this letter, however, he reveals nothing of Stanhope's changed nature, but remains loyal himself, pointing out instead how hardworking and tireless Stanhope is and that he is an excellent and well-respected officer. He finishes by telling his family of his pride in the knowledge that Stanhope is his friend.

On hearing that he is to help lead the raiding party, Raleigh is nervously enthusiastic. As the hour approaches, his nerves begin to dominate his enthusiasm and it is Osborne who comforts him. His youth and inexperience are revealed in this scene as he talks nervously to Osborne, trying not to dwell on the raid, refusing to have rum in his coffee and pointing out that he has never smoked a cigar before. This also emphasises the difference in age between the two men, with Raleigh seeming, more than ever, like the schoolboy while Osborne is the wise, kind and inspiring "school teacher".

After the raid, when Osborne is dead, Raleigh is clearly in shock and can barely stand up as he speaks to the Colonel. This new experience has made him understand the horror of the war - something which Stanhope had obviously wanted to spare him for as long as possible. Raleigh slowly comes to realise how much Osborne had meant to Stanhope. He feels left out of Stanhope's thoughts and doesn't understand his reactions. He wants to be involved and to help Stanhope, but cannot because his friend will not communicate with him. Raleigh would prefer to talk about his feelings, both for Osborne and for Stanhope, but Stanhope rejects this overture, angrily pushing Raleigh away.

There is an awkwardness between Raleigh and Stanhope because Raleigh had assumed that by being with Stanhope, everything would be as it was at school. He has also failed to understand that the war has changed Stanhope to such an extent - he remembers his friend as a young dashing officer, keen to join the fight, and barely recognises the man he has become. Stanhope, on the other hand, resents Raleigh's presence as a reminder of his old life and the person he once was. In addition, Stanhope has formed new friendships now, especially with Osborne, who he looks up to and respects. These are not the sort of feelings he can have for Raleigh whose innocence represents everything he has lost.

Ultimately, the only time that Raleigh is able to recapture the old Stanhope, is on his death-bed, as we get a glimpse of what their relationship once was. His hero looks after him and ensures that he feels safe, comfortable and unafraid.

Portrayal and Development of Raleigh

Sherriff had several purposes in creating the role of Raleigh. Firstly, he wanted to demonstrate the central theme of hero-worship - a subject which many in his audience would have related to quite easily. He also wanted to depict the immediate impact of war, to show that just one bad experience could change the character and perspective of a man. In this way, the audience not only gains a greater understanding of lost youth, but also of someone like Stanhope, who has seen so much more than Raleigh, but manages to survive.

Raleigh's presence is vital to the depiction of Stanhope's character, but he also represents a type of his own, namely the young men, who even late in the war had retained their eagerness and raw innocence, despite the lengthening casualty lists.

Raleigh's passage and the development of his character come about through a few separate episodes. Firstly he sees the change in Stanhope, which shocks him, but he remains loyal to his own friend. Then, when Raleigh writes his letter and is faced with Stanhope's anger (possibly for the first time in his life), he is stunned by the reaction he receives. Even then, he knows that deep down, Stanhope is still a decent man. The raid is really the turning point for Raleigh. It is his first experience of war and death, but his survival and Osborne's death provide the audience with some scenes of high emotion, between Raleigh and Stanhope, from which the young subaltern would possibly never have recovered. Stanhope's reaction to Osborne's death and his treatment of Raleigh change the dynamic of their friendship but, at the moment of his death, Sherriff allows Raleigh to see the return of his hero. He can die in peace, knowing that his friend did, indeed, care for and look after him until the end and that his faith in Stanhope was justified.

OSBORNE

General Description

While significantly older than Stanhope, Osborne is junior in rank. Married, with two children, he is physically tough and rugged - the opposite of his personality which is level-headed, friendly and trusting. His feelings for his family are clear when he tells Stanhope that he spent the whole of his last leave at home with them, not even going to see any shows. He describes with great warmth the peaceful evenings spent with his wife and playing at soldiers with his two sons. His choice of reading material is interesting: *Alice's Adventures in Wonderland* presumably reminds him of happier times at home. However, once he is back at the front, the Company become his family.

Character Analysis

Osborne is very protective of Stanhope, trying to help him wherever possible. Their relationship is not based on hero-worship: Osborne knows and appreciates Stanhope's faults but his respect for his senior officer is borne out of years of experience and time spent with Stanhope at the front. Osborne realises that being in command brings with it heavy responsibilities and he knows that these have taken their toll on Stanhope; despite this, however, Stanhope has remained an excellent and diligent officer, and it is this which earns him Osborne's love and respect. He defends Stanhope's actions to Raleigh and especially Hardy, showing his loyalty to his commanding officer.

Osborne is very kind to Raleigh, who is nervous when he first arrives. He tries to warn Raleigh that Stanhope has changed and also attempts to deflect Raleigh's hero-worship away from his old school friend, by pointing out that he had played rugby for Harlequins and England. This is not done in a boastful manner, but more as a means of diverting Raleigh's attention from Stanhope, who he knows will be troubled by Raleigh's presence. He is not a vain man which he demonstrates when Hardy suggests that he would make a better Commanding Officer than Stanhope - a suggestion which he adamantly refutes.

As a former school master, Osborne is used to looking after boys, and sees his position in the dugout as an extension of this role, to the point where he is nicknamed "Uncle". He is always on hand with sensible advice and words of wisdom and is keen to avoid conflict within the dugout. It is always Osborne who helps Stanhope, especially when he is drunk, or over-tired. His first concern is to protect his Commanding Officer from the prying eyes and judgement of others, but also from the most destructive influence in Stanhope's life - himself.

Osborne is very diplomatic: for example, his method of getting Mason to wash the dish-cloth is to ask his wife to send him out some soap powder and then suggest to Mason that he might like to try using it. Also when there is obviously a problem with Hibbert, Osborne deflects Trotter's enquiries and changes the subject.

His silences upon being told that he is to lead the raid, and his desire not to talk about it beforehand, demonstrate that he is wary of being sent on this mission. He is an officer of some experience and has been on raids before, but now he seems to have a sense of his own mortality as he gives his belongings to Stanhope for safe-keeping, to be returned to his wife should he not survive. He naturally overcomes his own nerves, at least for appearance's sake, and calms the nerves of Raleigh, who has never experienced anything like this before and, as the hour approaches, becomes more and more nervous. Osborne's attitude towards the men is always caring and considerate and although he is an officer of some standing, he has not yet become war-weary, like Stanhope. He has a sensible yet realistic perspective of the war.

Osborne's death signifies a change for this small group of officers. Raleigh, who was with him at the time, feels guilty and disturbed by Osborne's death, while Stanhope has lost the one fellow officer he knew he could trust implicitly. Even if the attack had not happened the next morning, one senses that this Company of men would never have been quite the same again.

Portrayal and Development of Osborne

Osborne is a pivotal personality in the play. Quite often it is through his eyes that the audience sees the traits of other characters. This is especially the case in the conversation between Osborne and Hardy about Stanhope. Here, not only do we discover that Stanhope is admired and respected by the men with whom he actually serves (as opposed to those who merely know him by reputation), but we also learn of Osborne's 'love' for Stanhope. His use of this word to describe his feelings shows his emotional maturity. He is not afraid to express himself or that he will be misunderstood; he knows and can explain, if necessary, that his love is platonic. He doesn't mind Hardy making fun of him, because he knows that his relationship with Stanhope is more important.

Raleigh's reactions to Stanhope are also enhanced by Osborne, who helps the new arrival to come to terms with the changes in his old school friend. Sherriff's portrayal of Osborne in this way allows the audience to see his respect for such officers, who provided a father-figure for their juniors, both in terms of age and rank. At the same time, we see that Sherriff is demonstrating the depth of emotion that was possible between the men in the trenches. Osborne is shown to be the 'glue' that holds this group of officers together and the consequences of his death threaten to split them apart.

Unlike some of the other characters, Osborne is not really shown to develop during the play, because he must be seen as the one stable force in the group, who guides the others through everything. Only in this way can Sherriff allow the audience to understand the feelings of loss that came with the death of such a valued man.

TROTTER

General Description

Trotter is obviously not in the best physical shape - he is rotund and red-faced. He is also middle-aged with a bursting tunic - the result, no doubt, of too much indulgence in his favourite interest - the consumption of food. He is married and his letters to his wife and descriptions of his home life, such as his garden, serve to remind us that all of these men have something to live for, and so much to lose.

Character Analysis

He is a friendly, tolerant character, who is supportive of his fellow officers and loyal to Stanhope. He is also concerned about Stanhope's drinking and health, although he does not have the same close relationship as his Commanding Officer shares with Osborne. Unlike the other officers, Trotter has been promoted through the ranks and, presumably, does not have the same public school background as them, which is demonstrated by the fact that his language is more colloquial than theirs. Outwardly, Trotter appears to be very unemotional, but the impression is given that this is only on the surface and that Trotter's feelings go much deeper than it would seem. In fact, when Stanhope says that he envies Trotter for being able to maintain a sense of normality, Trotter makes it clear that this is most definitely not the case. He doesn't like to talk about how he feels, using humour to overcome difficult circumstances, and therefore he falsely creates the impression that he doesn't feel anything.

Stanhope and Osborne, while liking Trotter, feel that he lacks imagination: they believe that they look more deeply at life, while he merely observes what is on the surface. This demonstrates one of the perceived differences between their classes. They have drive and ambition, while Trotter is happy with his lot in life. This is reinforced later on, when he points out that he has never owned a car, but that he and his wife used to walk everywhere together, but he does not seem to resent the fact that others have more than him.

Many critics describe Trotter as an artificial character - somewhat unnecessary to the plot. This does him a grave injustice as his importance lies in the subtleties of what he says: his reactions demonstrate the common feeling. So, for example, he's worried about the raid - even though he is not involved - but he knows that it is useless to argue, as the orders will not be revoked, no matter how pointless and costly the raid might be. He knows that nothing he can do will change the course of the war, but equally he does not see why he should have to suffer more discomfort than is absolutely necessary. Much of the humour in the play emanates from Trotter and centres on his love of food. Not only does he joke about things, but the others make fun of him, although this is never done offensively, but in friendship.

After Osborne's death, Trotter becomes Stanhope's second-in-command, but this brief relationship is more formal than Stanhope and Osborne's had been. Trotter feels honoured by the promotion and promises not to let Stanhope down. Even on the final morning, immediately before the attack, Trotter appears cheerful - he sings songs while in his dugout which helps to relieve the feeling of tension and probably also serves to take his own mind off what might lie ahead.

Portrayal and Development of Trotter

Sherriff portrays Trotter as the ordinary man, who has answered his country's call and gone to war to do his duty. By showing him as someone who has risen through the ranks, Sherriff is reminding the audience that many of the officers had actually come from working or middle class backgrounds, but had achieved the same status as the others through hard work. These men were given the somewhat unfair title of 'temporary gentlemen', suggesting that they were not really considered to be good enough to associate with the upper class officers on a permanent basis, while also reminding them that their position of 'gentleman' only held good for the duration of the war. By making Trotter such a good-natured and likeable man, Sherriff is probably expressing his distaste for this treatment of such men.

Sherriff uses Trotter to inject humour, but also humanity, into the play. Trotter is the mild-mannered, quiet and ordinary men, who represents the everyday person, seeing everything, but not necessarily commenting on it.

As the play progresses, Trotter's character develops a little. While he remains humorous, for the best part, right until the end, the audience is given greater and greater glimpses of the quieter and more thoughtful side of Trotter's nature. After Osborne's death, he does his best to help Stanhope, without trying to replace Osborne, even though his advice is not always welcomed. Initially, when we first see Trotter, the main focus of his attention is on food, but as time progresses, we see that he has a much deeper and more thoughtful personality, often showing his consideration for the other officers in quiet and unobtrusive ways.

HIBBERT

General Description

Hibbert is a young, slightly obscure man with a pale face, reminiscent of a weasel, both in appearance and manner. First impressions of Hibbert are not good. He complains of feeling unwell almost continuously and craves escape from the trenches.

Hibbert doesn't initially interact with his fellow-officers, although he knows them all well, preferring to sleep and keep his own company whenever he is not on duty, although one gets the impression that he does this to support his argument that he is unwell.

Character Analysis

During his quarrel with Stanhope, it becomes clear that Hibbert is terrified of going back into the trenches and is persuaded to stay only by Stanhope first threatening and then sympathising with him. This exchange shows Hibbert in an unfavourable light and although he agrees to stay, he then becomes concerned that Stanhope might tell the others of his cowardice. This confirms that Stanhope had been right in his assumption that Hibbert was faking his illness, and also shows that Hibbert is a shallow man whose sole concerns are his own welfare and reputation.

This bad impression is exacerbated by his reaction to Osborne's death. Whereas for Trotter and Stanhope, the meal and light conversation are a means to forget, Hibbert uses this opportunity to show off his lewd postcards and boast of his exploits with women - he simply wants to enjoy himself. He also gossips about Raleigh which shows he does not share the common sense of loyalty, which he seems to expect of others. Stanhope's distaste for Hibbert is obvious throughout the play, but really comes out in this scene.

When the time comes to go back into the trenches, he is again hesitant and fearful. In fact he has to be called several times before appearing on the morning of the final attack. He seems unwilling to go up into the trenches, wasting a great deal of time and making excuses, until Stanhope tells him to accompany Mason. This is Stanhope's way of shaming Hibbert into doing his duty - if Mason can do it, so can he. Although this works and Hibbert goes, he hesitates again and, unlike all the others, does not say anything to Stanhope.

Portrayal and Development of Hibbert

The portrayal of Hibbert is, perhaps, one of the most interesting aspects of the play. Most people have assumed, down the years, that Sherriff based the characters on people that he knew and met during the war and in most instances, this is the case. In his letters home from the trenches, he describes some of his fellow officers and some of their characteristics can be seen within the personalities included in the play, although they are almost all combinations of several different people. The case of Hibbert is no exception but the source for his inspiration is quite surprising. In some of his letters, Sherriff complains of having neuralgia and of making requests to be sent back down the line for treatment. He speaks of his fear and the fact that his nerves quite often get the better of him. Although he never shirked his duties, or showed off lewd postcards, it would seem that some of Hibbert's characteristics are autobiographical.

Hibbert's main purpose in the play is to show us how Stanhope reacts to being placed in difficult situations. In Hibbert's company, we see Stanhope angry, impatient, sympathetic, disgusted and irritated. Hibbert has a tendency to bring out the worst in others, but Stanhope still tries his best to show strong leadership, demonstrating understanding for Hibbert's nerves and fears. The audience is not necessarily supposed to sympathise with, or even like Hibbert: he is there to help us understand the traits of others and show how two different men, under the same stresses, will react in contrasting ways. As such, the audience grows to appreciate Stanhope even more.

Hibbert becomes even less likeable after Osborne's death and this development helps the audience to understand how much the loss of Osborne will affect the Company. Hibbert's behaviour is inappropriate and he shows himself to be selfish and inconsiderate, providing a good contrast with the other remaining officers.

Even at the end, Hibbert hasn't changed. He doesn't want to go up into the trench and tries to delay. Stanhope's reaction to this is the most important aspect, but the fact that they part without speaking shows that, despite his best efforts, Stanhope has achieved nothing in his attempts to make Hibbert a better, more considerate and more understanding officer. Within this depiction, Sherriff may well have been trying to reveal that, sometimes the war didn't alter or make men - sometimes they were just who they had always been.

MASON

General Description

Mason is essentially a servant and his general responsibility is to take care of the officers to whom he is assigned. He cooks their meals and clears up after them. This does not, however, mean that he escapes the fighting - he must also take part in any battles in which his company are involved.

Although we are told little about Mason's appearance or personality, we can conclude that he is hard-working, loyal and caring. He never questions his orders, and is keen to please. For example, prior to the final battle, he makes sandwiches for the officers, before going up into the trenches. Mason is often the butt of light-hearted jokes about food and cooking, but this is done without malice.

Character Analysis

Mason's job in the Company is to provide the meals for the officers, but his ability to do this is tempered by the ingredients which he is given. Although the other characters taunt him for this, the audience is given the impression that they are really grateful for his efforts.

Their gratitude is not limited to his cooking efforts. For example, when Stanhope suggests that Hibbert and Mason go up into the trench together, Mason appears pleased to have some company, which may demonstrate his own nervousness. This could, however, be interpreted as showing Mason's understanding of the real situation surrounding Hibbert and his desire to be useful to Stanhope. The audience sees Mason as someone who comes and goes throughout the play, not really getting involved in the main conversations, but this doesn't mean that he isn't fully aware of what is happening between the officers.

Portrayal and Development of Mason

The role of Mason's character in the play is to provide humourous respite in the building tension, his interactions with Trotter being particularly amusing. He also serves to remind us that, for the officers in the dugout, in spite of their surroundings and horrific experiences, ordinary activities still go on. The men must eat, and the discussion of what they are eating and how it has been cooked provides a useful diversion from the war, and in many cases, helps to enhance the human qualities of the play.

Although, for the main part of the play, Mason's role revolves around his kitchen duties, at the end we get to see that he must also fight and this serves to remind us that he is also still a soldier, with the same worries and fears as everyone else. Sherriff clearly wanted his audience to understand that the humour was a mask to allow Mason to get through each day.

HARDY

General Description

Hardy is a Captain, who commands the company from whom Stanhope's men are taking over. It would seem that he has been at the front for some time, as nothing really seems to surprise him.

Character Analysis and Portrayal of Hardy

Hardy's role in the play is to set the scene. His conversation with Osborne serves the purpose of explaining the anticipated attack, and Stanhope's personality, as well as some of the boredom and routine of trench-life.

Hardy is a humorous, philosophical character, who has a light-hearted outlook on almost everything, including the general hardships of the war, although this might be more obvious as he is being relieved and going behind the lines - whether he would be as amused if he were the one coming into the trenches is another matter.

This initial scene involving Hardy helps to set the tone for the rest of the play, and helps the reader or audience appreciate that this black humour was an important aspect of life in the trenches. During this scene, as well as learning about the still absent Stanhope, we also learn a great deal about Osborne and how well-respected he is amongst the other men - even those not in his own Company.

Relationships

Being as *Journey's End* is set entirely within the tight confines of a small dugout, the relationships portrayed between the characters involved become vitally important to the audience's understanding of the play. Some of the relationships are more crucial than others, but even the more minor ones can be used to help demonstrate some of the themes within this piece.

STANHOPE AND OSBORNE

This is probably the most important and complex relationship in the play. Osborne takes care of Stanhope, looking after him when he is drunk and making sure that he gets enough rest. He is also very protective of Stanhope, defending his behaviour to Hardy and explaining that Stanhope's experiences have made him the way he is. During Osborne's conversation with Hardy, he makes it clear that Stanhope keeps nothing from him. Hardy reveals an episode that he considers to be embarrassing and detrimental to Stanhope, and is then surprised when Osborne explains that he was already aware of what had taken place because Stanhope had told him all about it himself. The trust between Osborne and Stanhope is obvious from that moment on and is enhanced by the fact that Stanhope later shares his fears that Raleigh will write home to his family and tell them how much Stanhope has changed. Again Osborne shows his concern, explaining that Raleigh wouldn't do this and trying to calm Stanhope's worries.

Although Stanhope is the senior officer and has seen more service, he doesn't really issue Osborne with orders in the same way as the other men and treats him as more of an equal. Because Osborne is older, he takes on the role of father-figure, offering sound advice to Stanhope whenever he over-reacts. At the same time, Osborne looks up to Stanhope, appreciating his qualities as an officer and leader, while realising that he always puts everyone else ahead of himself. It is this mutual respect and affection which makes this relationship more interesting and realistic.

Even though Osborne holds Stanhope in high esteem, he is not always full of praise for his captain's actions and Stanhope doesn't simply bow down to everything that Osborne says. When Stanhope first mentions censoring Raleigh's letter, Osborne is taken aback. Both men know that Stanhope has every right to do this, but Osborne feels that it shows an unjustified lack of trust in Stanhope's former schoolfriend. The real crunch comes when Raleigh has actually written his letter and Stanhope snatches it from him, using an unnecessary amount of force. Afterwards, Osborne reads Raleigh's letter aloud to Stanhope, not to prove him wrong, so much as to show him that he should have more faith - not only in Raleigh, but also in himself. Osborne's protective attitude towards Stanhope comes out in this scene. He could just have left the letter for Stanhope to read alone, but he really wanted Stanhope to realise the consequences of continuing to push Raleigh away.

There is a strong emotional connection between the two men which is made clear right at the very beginning of the play when Osborne explains to Hardy that he loves Stanhope. This is not a homosexual love and neither is it as simple as the love between two friends. The bonds formed in the trenches were often more powerful and the relationships stronger than even those between a husband and wife and that is the type of 'love' which Osborne is describing here. He is being quite serious when he comments that he would 'go to hell' with Stanhope and the strength of their relationship is made more obvious by the descriptions of Osborne's time with his family, which is given the air of something more comforting and homely, rather than being as powerful and intense as his time with Stanhope.

Stanhope's fear of losing Osborne is made clear before the raid as he wonders 'what [he] would do' without his 'Uncle', while only grudgingly accepting Osborne's belongings to pass on to his wife, refusing to acknowledge that Osborne might not survive. There is a slightly lighthearted tone to this scene, but the undercurrent is highly emotional, as deep down, both men understand the seriousness of the situation, even though neither really wants to face it. Osborne's death is devastating for Stanhope, to the point where he can't bear to see Raleigh sitting on Osborne's bed. Although Stanhope joins in the dinner with Trotter and Hibbert that evening, he does so to 'forget', not to celebrate or remember and he later flares up at Raleigh, explaining vehemently that by Osborne's death he has lost 'the one man [he] could trust', the man who 'understood everything', who he considered as his 'best friend'.

Sherriff's portrayal of this relationship is especially useful in demonstrating the strength of feelings which were felt between the men in the trenches. The trust which developed was rarely found elsewhere and nowhere within the play can this be seen any better. The relationship between Stanhope and Osborne also shows the family element of the play in that Osborne is very much the father-figure, as well as being everyone's 'Uncle'. Although he is not the senior officer, he is very much the one to whom everyone looks for advice and good sense and, despite the fact that Stanhope is his senior, he does not resent the respect shown to Osborne.

Although it could be argued that we do not really see a development in this relationship, that might be because we don't really need to. The strength of feeling between the two men is already so powerful and remains so until the end. The only real development required, therefore, is the feeling of loss which Stanhope has to suffer after Osborne's death, which is made palpable by his need to forget and also by his reactions to his old schoolfriend, Raleigh.

STANHOPE AND RALEIGH

Of all the relationships in Journey's End, the one between Stanhope and Raleigh is the only one which has any basis outside of the war and the confines of the play itself. At school, with Stanhope having been a few years older than Raleigh and a popular, sporting student, the younger boy had looked up to Stanhope as his hero. Raleigh's arrival in Stanhope's Company takes him by surprise, but this emotion soon turns to fear, laced with anger, as Stanhope reveals to Osborne his concern that Raleigh will write to his sister and tell her how much Stanhope has changed. The prospect of this is upsetting for Stanhope, as is the idea that he must crush Raleigh's perceptions of him as a hero. Stanhope appreciates that Raleigh's presence will place him under even more strain as not only must he try to appear normal to the youngster, but he still feels the need to protect him. This aspect comes to the fore when the Colonel proposes that Raleigh should accompany Osborne on the raid. Stanhope had made no comment about sending Osborne out, but when Raleigh's name is suggested, he objects, making excuses as to why he shouldn't go.

Raleigh is very naive about his relationship with Stanhope and expects it to be just as it was at school. He thinks that their previous connection and shared memories still count for something because he doesn't realise the strain that Stanhope is under or how much the war has changed him. The hero-worship that Stanhope feels for Raleigh doesn't really diminish, placing even more pressure on Stanhope, although a lot of this is self-imposed as Stanhope sets himself very high standards.

There are two episodes that change the relationship between Raleigh and Stanhope. The first is their exchange over Raleigh's letter; the second is Osborne's death. When Raleigh withdraws his letter because he doesn't want Stanhope to read it, Stanhope automatically assumes the worst - that Raleigh has written to Madge, telling her of his downfall. Stanhope's angry reaction stuns Raleigh and, for the first time, he really sees Stanhope in a new light. Of course, once Stanhope realises that Raleigh has only written in praise of him and that his reluctance of have his letter censored was due to embarrassment, he appreciates that his reaction has now caused precisely the damage he had been hoping to avoid. Any chance Stanhope might have had of retaining Raleigh's inspired good opinion is now lost and he regrets his outburst on many levels. After this episode, Raleigh becomes a little more guarded in his attitude towards Stanhope.

Osborne's death has an even more dramatic effect on this relationship. Stanhope's response is surprising to Raleigh, in that he joins the other officers in a special meal. Raleigh, meanwhile, chooses to remain in the trench with the men, sharing their rations. Raleigh's actions anger Stanhope, but equally the younger man cannot understand how Stanhope can laugh and drink following the death of his friend. This episode highlights the differences that exist between the two men and how much their relationship has changed since they were at school. When Stanhope reveals his true feelings for Osborne, Raleigh is lost. For the first time, he realises that Stanhope is not as strong as he had thought an that he needs people too. The fact that Stanhope has now lost the man he needed most also makes Raleigh understand how he would feel if something happened to Stanhope.

At the very end of the play, the audience is finally given a glimpse of the relationship between the two men, as Raleigh remembers it and as Stanhope wishes it could have been. Stanhope is shown to be gentle, kind and considerate, as well as heroic. His grief for Raleigh is obvious and his feelings show through even after Raleigh has died and he is briefly left alone with his thoughts. Raleigh is shown as naive and innocent, completely dependent on his friend who - no matter the personal cost - never fails him.

STANHOPE AND HIBBERT

The relationship between Stanhope and Hibbert is very different to the ones between Stanhope and Osborne or Raleigh. This is not a friendly relationship, which would stand the test of time outside of the trenches; it is much more professional and is based on the need for them to interact as two soldiers, rather than a wish, on the part of either of them, for any kind of friendship. Even from their first conversation, the audience is made awre of the tension between these two. Hibbert's first comments relate to his attempts to prove that he is not well enough to remain in the front lines and although Stanhope tries to jolly him along, Hibbert holds fast to his excuses. Only once Hibbert is out of earshot do we discover what Stanhope really thinks of him, in that he describes him to Osborne as a 'little worm'. Stanhope is determined that Hibbert will do his duty and this becomes obvious in the argument between the two men. Stanhope is initially angry about Hibbert's attitude and threatens to shoot him, but only to avoid the 'disgrace' of an inevitable court martial. It is only when Hibbert stands up to the threat made by Stanhope that the senior officer explains his own fears, eventually making Hibbert understand that he has obligations to himself and his fellow officers and then the atmosphere between them calms. Stanhope offers to help Hibbert and seems to have earned his respect.

After Osborne's death, Stanhope just wants to get drunk so that he can forget about his personal loss, while Hibbert uses the opportunity of the dinner to have a good time and show off. He goes too far with is boasting and making comments about Raleigh, which leads Stanhope to become angry and break up the party. This shows the relationship as it really is: no matter how hard Stanhope tries to tolerate and accommodate Hibbert, they will never really be able to get along. The final parting between the two men only reinforces their differences in that Stanhope is forced to get Mason to accompany Hibbert into the trenches and can barely conceal his impatience with the junior officer.

Sherriff's portrayal of this relationship serves the purpose of demonstrating more about the personalities involved, especially Hibbert as he rarely speaks to any great extent with the other characters. By Stanhope's reactions, we can appreciate how cowardly Hibbert's behaviour is, but also how the same circumstances and feelings bring out different reactions in the two men. This portrayal makes the audience more accepting and sympathetic towards Stanhope, despite his obvious problems, while it is made difficult to feel anything other than contempt for Hibbert.

Initially, after the argument over Hibbert's neuralgia, the audience might be lulled into thinking that the relationship between Stanhope and Hibbert could change into something more positive. However, the scenes at the dinner following Osborne's death reveal that deep down, nothing has changed. As far as Stanhope - and the audience - is concerned, Hibbert was a 'worm' at the beginning of the play and he is a 'worm' at the end.

TROTTER AND MASON

This is a very different relationship to all the others portrayed in the play, especially in that it is between an officer and a ranking soldier. The fact that Mason has a more familiar relationship with Trotter than with the other officers probably stems from the fact that they come from similar backgrounds. Although Trotter is an officer, he has risen through the ranks and would at the time have been classified as a 'temporary gentleman'. This status would ordinarily have made it quite difficult for him to fit in anywhere: his fellow officers might well have perceived him as being beneath them, while the ordinary soldiers could easily have felt as though he had ideas above his station. The relationships between Mason and Trotter works because they have something in common - namely food.

The conversations between these two characters demonstrate how, even in the trenches, with the tension of an impending attack, the normal, everyday things of life, such as what would be served for dinner, or why there was no pepper to go with the soup, were still important. Indeed, it could be said that these matters actually took on a greater significance at such times, not only because they served as a diversion, but also because they provided a reminder of home at a time when it must have felt very distant.

The purpose of the relationship between Trotter and Mason is to provide a domesticated element, which would help the audience to realise that the characters were really just ordinary men, placed into extraordinary circumstances. More importantly, perhaps, it also injects some humour into the play, without which it would be much less effective. Their interactions help to lighten what would otherwise be quite a dark and subdued piece, in which the only conversations would take place between officers, mainly from the same backgrounds, making the play more one dimensional. Sherriff's introduction of this relationship and the shared humour between these characters gives the whole play a different and more human emphasis.

HISTORICAL SIGNIFICANCE

The historical setting of the play is significant and accurate. The play starts on March 18th 1918 which was three days before the Germans launched "Operation Michael" at St Quentin.

This was Germany's attempt to end the war before the Americans could arrive in any great number and therefore tip the balance of power in favour of the Allies. Germany, like most of the countries involved in the First World War, was running out of men of military age and the success of this attack was therefore vital.

General Erich Ludendorff declared that the object of this attack must be a resounding victory over the British and the selection of the place for the proposed attack was therefore, of great importance. Immediately in front of the St Quentin trenches was the old Somme battlefield. This was difficult terrain which consisted of water-logged shell-holes and abandoned trenches. Ludendorff thought that, both tactically and psychologically, this was the ideal place to strike. The intention was that, by use of specialist storm troops, the German army would punch a hole in the British front line, and force a retreat towards the coast. However, Ludendorff had no fixed idea as to what would follow this initial strike.

The first days of this battle were extremely bloody and losses on both sides were heavy. It would not be surprising, therefore, if all the characters in *Journey's End* died, since the bombardment and subsequent attack resulted in many British deaths. As a result of these initial losses and the speed of the German advance, the Allied armies became separated which resulted in arguments between Haig (Commander in Chief of the British Army) and Pétain (his equivalent in the French force). At a hastily convened meeting the Allies decided to have one Supreme Commander, which it was decided should be Marshal Ferdinand Foch. This was a significant step and enabled the Allies to fight in a more co-ordinated fashion, with reserves and weaponry being better deployed.

Germany failed to exploit her initial successes and rather than continuing with the plan of a single-pronged attack, her forces became divided. In addition, the selection of the old Somme battleground now seemed unwise as it proved to be difficult terrain for an attacking army to advance over. In addition, the Germans had advanced much further than their lines of supply could support, so by 5th April the German High Command were forced to admit that Operation Michael had achieved as much as could be expected, and further attacks in this area were abandoned.

Before long, American troops began to arrive and this had a great demoralising effect on the German army. Attacks continued at other points on the front and it would take many more months, and many many more deaths before the war was over.

Field Marshal
Sir Douglas Haig

General
Henri-Philippe Pétain

Marshal
Ferdinand Foch

Photo Credits: Photo's of the Great War

The ruins of St Quentin.
Photo Credit: Photo's of the Great War

Entrance to St Quentin canal tunnel under the ridge at Bellicourt, on the Hindenburg Line.
Photo Credit: Photo's of the Great War

RANKS IN THE BRITISH ARMY

Some students find the named ranks and their responsibilities difficult to interpret. The following provides a very brief outline of the role of each of the ranks involved in *Journey's End*.

COLONEL

The most senior officer involved in the play, the Colonel is, in all probability, in charge of a battalion of over 1000 men, divided into four companies. The company involved in Journey's End is 'C' Company. During the course of the war, with the influx of the New Armies and the number of casualties the quantity of men in a battalion varied widely.

CAPTAIN

This rank belongs to the characters of both Stanhope and Hardy. These men are both in charge of companies of approximately 230 men. They are responsible for the maintenance of their area of trench, as well as the morale and physical well-being of the men under their command. It is their duty to ensure that the men are in a fit state to undertake whatever tasks they must perform - whether that involves fighting in battle or 'fatigues' (manual labour, such as clearing roads, digging trenches etc.)

LIEUTENANTS AND SECOND LIEUTENANTS

These ranks apply to all the other officers in the play. It may fairly be assumed that Osborne is superior in rank to Trotter, Hibbert and Raleigh, as he is Stanhope's second-in-command, so he probably holds the rank of Lieutenant, while the others are Second-Lieutenants. Their responsibilities were essentially to help their captain in maintaining the day-to-day running of the company. In addition, each of these men would have been responsible for a Platoon within the company, consisting of approximately 50 men each.

COMPANY SERGEANT-MAJOR

This rank is held by the most senior non-commissioned officer in a company. A commissioned officer being one who has been charged, or 'commissioned' into a specific position. The CSM is, generally speaking, responsible for standards and discipline amongst the lower ranks. Beneath him there would be other sergeants and the men. In times of battle the CSM is responsible for seeing to the safe removal of the wounded and dealing with prisoners

OTHER RANKS

These include Sergeants, Corporals, Lance Corporals and Privates. The only named 'other rank' in the play is Mason, the officer's servant, who in this role would be the only soldier, other than the officers, to spend much time in the dugout.

R C SHERRIFF - BIOGRAPHY

Robert Cedric Sherriff was born on 6th June 1896 in Hampton Wick, near Kingston upon Thames in Surrey. He had an older sister, Beryl, and a younger brother, Cecil and their father, Herbert worked as an insurance clerk. Their mother, Annie Constance (née Winder) would almost certainly have met their father as a result of her family being neighbours of Herbert's brother John, when he left home, having married his wife, Bertha and moved away from the family home in Mortlake to nearby Barnes, just a few doors down from the Winder residence.

Robert was educated at Kingston Grammar School, before following his father into Sun Insurance, as a clerk on a salary of 15 shillings per week. Both his father and his grandfather had worked for this company and there had never really been any question of Robert doing anything else, although he and his father had harboured ambitions of Robert going to Oxford university, had the family's finances permitted. So, Robert settled down to a quiet, if rather dull life, commuting to the London office and working at a desk all day.

Once war was declared, Sherriff waited until after his nineteenth birthday and enlisted on November 20th 1915 in the Artists' Rifles, beginning his training at Hare Hall, Gidea Park in Essex. He wrote many letters home and was quite introspective and lonely during this time, presumably missing his family. Once his initial training was complete, Sherriff was commissioned as a Second Lieutenant and attached to the 9th Battalion of the East Surrey Regiment. He was sent for further training to Grand Shaft Barracks at Dover. From here, he embarked for France, arriving on Thursday 28th September and, within four days, had been placed in charge of a platoon of 25 men in the reserve lines, awaiting their orders to move up to the front. His first experience of front-line duty took place on 11th October, but after only four days, Sherriff's letters show that he was already beginning to feel the strain, partly due to lack of sleep. Despite this, Sherriff still found the time to appreciate his surroundings, wondering at their wrecked beauty, shattered by the repeated shelling. During the months of November and December, Sherriff was seconded to the Royal

Engineers for a tunnelling course, but upon his return, discovered that he would have to wait a further six months before being allowed any leave. He was enormously disappointed, but to pass the time, created a chart on which he could count off the passing days.

Towards the end of January 1917, Sherriff became unwell, suffering from neuralgia around his left eye and on 26th of the month, was transferred to an Officer's Rest Station behind the lines. Throughout the spring, the neuralgia returned sporadically, until he was granted a much needed ten days of leave at the end of June, returning to the trenches on 4th July. At the end of the month, he participated in the beginning of the Third Battle of Ypres, also known as Passchendaele, and a couple of days later, on 2nd August, was wounded in the face and hand, earning himself a "Blightly", so that by mid-August, he was settled in hospital at Netley in Hampshire. Although Sherriff expected to be declared fit again fairly soon, his neuralgia flared up again and he was transferred to St Thomas's Hospital in London. From there, once well, he returned to Dover, where he was employed in the training of new recruits. In March 1918, Sherriff was promoted to the rank of Lieutenant but, while waiting to be sent overseas again that summer, contracted influenza. By the time he was sufficiently recovered, the war was over, although he was promoted to the rank of Captain in January 1919.

With the war over, Sherriff returned to his job at Sun Insurance, although he gave up his desk job and went out on the road, dealing with claims and new policies, preferring the freedom that this role afforded him. To fill his spare time, Sherriff joined the nearby Kingston Rowing Club, which gave him an outlet for physical exercise, as well as the sense of belonging that he had enjoyed in the army. In 1921, the club discovered that it was in need of some new equipment and boat repairs and decided to put on an evening's entertainment in the form of sketches, musical features and a one-act play which Sherriff undertook to write. This he entitled A Hitch in the Proceedings and it was such a resounding success that the club launched the Adventurer's Dramatic Society, making their performances an annual event. Eventually they dropped the other acts and featured full three-act plays written entirely by Sherriff. This carried on for a further five years, three of which Sherriff also spent as Club captain, before he decided to give up the rowing club.

This decision meant that Sherriff found his evenings empty once again and he decided to put forward one of his rowing club plays to a London agent, selecting Curtis Brown for the purpose. He sent them his rowing club play Profit and Loss, which they liked, but rejected. He tried again, with another entitled

Cornlow on the Downs, which was once again returned. Sherriff didn't feel that his other plays were so good, and chose to turn his hand to novel writing instead. Several years earlier, he had thought up a plot based around hero-worship which featured two schoolboys: Dennis Stanhope, a popular, sporty, attractive hero; and Jimmy Raleigh, a bit of a plodder, who worships Stanhope. Upon leaving school Stanhope drifts along hopelessly, trying to live on his wits, while Raleigh does well, becoming a successful businessman. Raleigh wants to help his old schoolboy hero, but Stanhope resents every attempt that Raleigh makes. Despite having a plot outline, however, Sherriff found his own limited vocabulary a bit of an issue when it came to novel writing and before long, abandoned this idea.

As the evenings dragged on, Sherriff began to wonder whether he might be able to turn the story of Stanhope and Raleigh into a play, possibly making it more attractive to the agents by the addition of a war setting or background. Before long, this idea had taken hold and Sherriff had decided to set the entire play in a dugout, basing the characters on people he had met and the dialogue on his own experiences. It took a year to write, but when complete, Sherriff had only to find a title. He thought first of "Suspense", but rejected this as misleading; then he tried "Waiting", but thought this too commonplace. One night, while reading a book, he came upon the words: "It was late in the evening when we came at last to our Journey's End" and knew that he had found his title.

Curtis Brown responded well to the manuscript, and eventually the Incorporated Stage Society said they would put on the play on the 9th/10th December for two performances at the Apollo Theatre in London. They offered the production to a virtually known director, James Whale, and fully expected it to fail. Whale managed to procure the services of 21 year old Laurence Olivier - then an unknown actor - to play the part of Stanhope and it was agreed that all of the actors would be as little known as possible, allowing the audience to focus on the characters, rather than the men playing them. Many of the props and outfits were borrowed, with Olivier using Sherriff's uniform, which only needed the addition of an MC ribbon.

The opening performance went well, as did the second and received excellent reviews, but Sherriff's natural euphoria was short-lived: no theatre managers were interested in picking up the play. Then, on December 23rd, Sherriff was approached by Maurice Browne, who said he would produce Journey's End at the Savoy Theatre, with Whale directing. The play opened on 21st January with the same cast, except for Laurence Olivier, who had been given the lead role in Beau Geste at His Majesty's Theatre, but who was ably replaced by Colin Clive.

Again, the play was a resounding success, and ran for eighteen months, transferring to the Prince of Wales Theatre when the Savoy closed for refurbishment. It was translated into 27 languages and performed around the world, enabling Sherriff to eventually relinquish his job at Sun Insurance. His new-found fame brought him into contact with other literary notables, including H. G. Wells, Somerset Maugham, Ivor Novello, Rebecca West and, eventually two of his greatest heroes, Rudyard Kipling and J. M. Barrie. In 1930, the play was made into a film in Hollywood with James Whale directing, but back in England, people were clamouring for Sherriff's next play. After a few false starts, he wrote a story of English village life, entitled Badger's Green, which failed dismally to entice either critics or audiences.

This failure caused Sherriff a few financial problems. While Journey's End was at the height of its success, he had earned well and had bought a house at Esher in Surrey called Rosebriars. Once furnished, the total cost of this purchase came to around £10,000 and he needed an income of approximately £5,000 per year to maintain the property, but once Journey's End closed, and Badger's Green failed, he was only earning about one quarter of this. He needed another success. With his capital dwindling, Sherriff decided to enrol at university, with a view to becoming a schoolmaster. After one unsuccessful interview, Sherriff was accepted, in 1931, at New College, Oxford and that summer, while waiting to go up, decided to write a novel, entitled The Fortnight in September, which met with great critical acclaim and sold in tens of thousands.

In Autumn 1931, Sherriff rented a small house in Oxford, which he shared with his mother, and began his studies in history. He also rekindled his keen interest in rowing, having been a member of the Leander Club, and was welcomed with open arms by the college eight, rowing at number 7. At the end of the season, the captain informed Sherriff that he would be recommending him the following year for a place in the University crew: Sherriff, at the age of 36 would have the opportunity to earn a coveted Oxford Blue.

In the spring of 1932, Sherriff received a surprise letter from James Whale, who was now working for Universal Pictures in Hollywood, inviting Sherriff to go to America to write the screenplay for The Invisible Man by H. G. Wells. Although Sherriff was very tempted by this kind and lucrative offer, he also still felt drawn to Oxford and the chance of his Blue, as well as acknowledging his indebtedness to the warden of New College for allowing him to study there as a Special Student in the first place. The warden came to his rescue, suggesting that Sherriff take an elongated summer break, go to Hollywood and return to Oxford the following autumn.

So, in spring 1932, Sherriff and his mother travelled to Hollywood, where he worked diligently on the screenplay, avoided the loud, late-night parties, but enjoyed quiet and entertaining dinners with Charlie Chaplin, Ronald Colman, Boris Karloff and Norma Shearer among many others. When the job was done, Universal offered him a very profitable contract to stay on in Hollywood, which he declined, recalling not only his promise to the warden, but also the coveted Oxford Blue that might still be his. Sherriff and his mother returned to England, arriving in Liverpool on August 12th 1932.

Autumn saw Sherriff back on the river, practising hard to get back into shape. He did well, getting through the first two trials, before becoming ill. He was diagnosed with pleurisy and ordered to rest. Sherriff's disappointment was complete when he was later informed that he would definitely have been selected for the Oxford crew, had his health not failed him. More bad news followed, in a meeting between Sherriff and his tutor, in which the latter pointed out that Sherriff would be lucky to scrape a pass and might even fail his degree, but would certainly not achieve the honours required to become a schoolmaster. Sherriff was philosophical in his disappointment: he had gained a great deal from his Oxford experience and would always be grateful for the opportunity. He was only half-sad, therefore, to pick up his pen and write to Universal Pictures, who had left their offer open, suggesting in doing so, that he could work from home, rather than in Hollywood.

Writing in England and sending the scripts to America was more difficult than Sherriff had imagined and, after two failed screenplays, he and Universal parted company. Sherriff began to worry that he'd taken a wrong turn in leaving Oxford, when he was approached by studio owner Alexander Korda, who was building his own facility at Denham in Buckinghamshire. He wanted Sherriff to write the screenplay for The Four Feathers by A E W Mason, which proved to be another resounding success. This was followed by Goodbye Mr Chips, written for MGM, for which Sherriff was Oscar-nominated.

Despite his movie successes, Sherriff longed to return to his first-love in the theatre and, with actress Jeanne de Casalis wrote St Helena, based on the final day of Napolean Bonaparte. After a faltering start, this turned into another success at the Old Vic. Sherriff, now financially more secure, spent the next three years from 1936 to 1939 setting up and funding an archaeological dig at Angmering in Sussex, where the remains of a Roman villa had been discovered. He found this a thoroughly enjoyable and rewarding experience, brought to an end only by the beginning of the Second World War.

Initially, Sherriff was employed by the Ministry of Information to write propaganda and also to help recruit people into joining the A.R.P. Then in spring 1940, Korda contacted him again, wanting another screenplay - this time for Lady Hamilton (also known as That Hamilton Woman). After a very difficult journey, Sherriff and his mother arrived in Hollywood, where he was pleased to renew his acquaintance with Laurence Olivier who was going to star in the film, alongside his new wife, Vivien Leigh. Once production was complete, Sherriff worked on Mrs Miniver and then This Above All. He wanted to return to England, but it was impossible to secure a passage without a good reason, so Korda provided him with a contract that required him to be in London. Just as Sherriff and his mother were about to depart, the Japanese attacked Pearl Harbour, throwing everyone on the West coast into a state of panic. They had to wait for a safe passage and didn't end up returning to England until 7th August 1944 on board the Cunard ship Rangitata.

After the war, Sherriff began to tire of screenwriting and, after a fifteen year gap, decided to write another play. This was the story of a kindly, poor spinster who murders her wealthy mean, widowed sister, so that she can pass her money onto worthy causes. Sherriff entitled the play Miss Mable and it went on at The Duchess Theatre becoming a triumph, and running for six months. Thus inspired, Sherriff wrote Home at Seven, which was performed at The Wyndham's Theatre with Ralph Richardson in the lead role. He scored another hit, the play running for 342 performances in the West End.

Sherriff then wrote a play called The Long Sunset, in the mid 1950s. The inspiration for this came from his time at Angmering excavating the Roman villa and told the story of a Roman family living in Britain. He offered the play to the BBC for their Saturday Night Theatre slot, through which it reached a radio audience of around five million listeners. It was then performed at the Birmingham Repertory Theatre and Bernard Miles put it on at the Mermaid Theatre in London. The Cambridge examining board chose the text as the Modern English play for their English examination that year. Schools flocked to the theatre and Sherriff gave talks prior to the performances.

Then, quite unexpectedly Hollywood resurfaced, offering Sherriff something that he considered as "the best": the screenplay for The Dambusters. With this under his belt, the world was his oyster and he wrote further novels, plays and screenplays until the theatre became too modern and readers tired of his style of writing: there were younger - but not necessarily better - men to fill his shoes, and he reluctantly passed the baton to them.

Sherriff lived quietly at Rosebriars in Esher until his death on 13th November 1975. He bequeathed his house to Elmbridge Borough Council for social and cultural purposes and the money raised from the sale of the property established the R C Sherriff Rosebriars Trust which still exists today, promoting and assisting the arts in the Borough of Elmbridge.

PERFORMANCE FEATURES

In looking at performance techniques, students can examine not only the intention of the original playwright, but also how the play is adapted and interpreted by other directors. The playwright's ideas or instructions are usually written down within the script and, in the case of *Journey's End*, Sherriff has been quite precise as to how and where everything should be positioned and the movement and actions of the characters.

When looking at the interpretations of more modern directors, this can only be done when a performance of the play has actually been seen, which is not always possible. I was able to see a production of *Journey's End* in 2008, which was, in many ways, quite different to the one envisaged by Sherriff. However, this enables me to, hopefully, provide some useful insight for students.

SETTING

Journey's End is set entirely in a dugout during the few days prior to the German Spring Offensive which began on 21st March 1918. In the play, Sherriff gave specific instructions as to how the dugout should look, including the layout and style of the furniture and the 'magazine pictures pinned to the wall of girls in flimsy costumes'. His own experiences provided him with the background knowledge to make this setting as realistic as possible and thus create the required tension needed within this confined space. The presence of the war is really quite remote to the audience, who in the original play only heard its sounds 'faint and far away'.

In a modern version of the play, the director would normally adhere to broadly these same guidelines, although they could, of course, move things around somewhat. The other differences could include the use of projections above or behind the dugout scene to give the audience an idea of what is taking place in the trenches.

LIGHTING

Sherriff's directions include lighting from the outside in the form of moonlight and Very lights, as well as a 'pale shaft of sunlight' in the morning scenes. Within the dugout, there are candles on the table. In this way, the impression can be created that anyone not seated at the table is in semi-darkness. With the use of theatre lights, this element can be enhanced to suit the mood of particular scenes.

In a modern production, it is significantly easier to make use of lighting effects, which may be employed to generate an atmosphere of tension or high emotion. A perfect example of this could be the scene when Raleigh dies in which only that area of the stage is lit, while the remainder is left in comparative darkness. Once Raleigh has died and Stanhope is alone, the director then focuses a single light on him, leaving Raleigh in subdued shadow, so the audience know that he is still there, but are concentrating on Stanhope's expressions and reactions.

SOUND EFFECTS

Being as the audience of the original production could never actually see anything to do with the action of the war, the sound effects were very important in creating an authentic atmosphere. This is especially the case during the raid, when nothing is actually happening on the stage. Everything is left to the audience's imagination at this point and given the events that are to follow, it is important that the raid should sound as dramatic as possible.

More modern productions can take advantage of different forms of sound effects and mindle these with visual and graphic elements to create something more dramatic, but probably less realistic. Music can also be used, although this is not always appropriate and can sometimes detract from the audience's concentration on a specific moment in the play.

NON-VERBAL COMMUNICATIONS

Regardless of when the play is produced, the power and quality of the non-verbal communications is of vital importance. These will quite often take the form of looks, glances and meaningful silences between two or more characters and can, if handled well by both directors and actors, speak volumes. There are moments where 'eyes meet' between two characters, most notably at the time when Stanhope and Osborne part company and when Osborne and Raleigh are about to go on the raid. These small devices create an emotional link between the characters which words could not have done, mainly because in such as situation, these men would have shied away from saying what they really felt, but could express it with one simple look.

COSTUMES AND PROPS

In the original production, most of the costumes and props were either improvised or borrowed. So, for example, Laurence Olivier, as Stanhope, wore Sherriff's army uniform. Sherriff had been a captain in the war, so the only addition needed was an MC ribbon to make it perfect for Stanhope.

Modern productions often make use of purpose-made, rather than original, uniforms and props, which are perfectly adequate from the perspective of the audience. Occasionally a director may choose to inject a little modernity into the production, but in the case of *Journey's End*, this rarely works.

ENDING

According to the directions given, the play ends with Stanhope leaving the dugout and, as a shell lands nearby, the 'timber props of the roof cave slowly in'. The stage is in darkness with only the occasional light of the coming dawn showing through the cracks of the 'broken doorway'. In the distance, machine-gun and rifle fire can be heard. Being as no other directions are given, we may assume that at this point, the curtain fell.

The ending of the play is something with which modern directors have been able to meddle. While the departure of Stanhope must, essentially, remain the same, directors are free to change what happens next. Some miss out the destruction of the dugout, drop the curtain and project a poignant scene, such as poppies. Others simply leave the stage in darkness. In the production which I saw, the ending was especially well handled. After Stanhope had mounted the steps and the gunfire had ceased, the Last Post was sounded. The stage was darkened and the cast marched out to stand in a dim light at the front of the stage in one line, facing the audience. At this point, the audience began to applaud. Then the actor playing the Company Sergeant Major stepped forward and, in a voice raised above the applause, gave the order to salute, before dismissing the Company. They didn't bow, or even acknowledge the audience, but remained in character and it really felt as though they were saluting and individually paying tribute to the men they had been portraying.

THEMES

FUTILITY AND WASTE

Journey's End is now generally recognised as an anti-war play, although some historians doubt that this was Sherriff's original intention. Some confusion, it would seem, arose from a difference of opinion between Sherriff and the play's original producer. Sherriff's intention was, rather, to portray the pride which the men felt in each other and the comradeships which developed in such difficult circumstances. In doing so, he also demonstrates the human cost of the war, in that the men seem to be required to give their lives - and even those who survived would never be the same again - for no reason. Death is indiscriminate, taking those who least deserve to fall, and these deaths are seen to serve little or no purpose. The men are generally portrayed as worthy people who have accepted their presence in the war as something they had to do - a necessary evil. Although the men, especially Stanhope, may question the value of activities such as the raid, none of them speak out against the war itself, despite the fact that it costs them all dearly.

These themes are best demonstrated immediately before and after the raid, led by Osborne and Raleigh. The purpose of this raid is to capture some German soldiers to find out where the anticipated attack is likely to take place, and the strength and nature of the opposing army. The colonel points out, somewhat optimistically, that the success of this raid may constitute an early end to the war. However, the discovery of the type of opposition you are facing is unlikely to affect the outcome of a battle, if you have nothing more to throw at it yourself. Therefore, it would seem that the colonel is seeking to justify the raid, when in fact, as Stanhope suggests, there can be no justification for such a waste of lives. The raiding party manages to capture a young German soldier, whose limited information is greeted with disproportionate pleasure by the Colonel. He appears to feel that the raid has accomplished its aims. The details given by the captured German soldier, however, seem insignificant compared with the loss of life necessitated during his seizure.

The deaths of Osborne and six of the men accompanying him, is a great price for this Company to pay. For Osborne - surely the most likeable character in the play - to have died at all is lamentable, but to have died for so little and in such circumstances is tragic - a point which Stanhope grasps, and which makes him bitter and angry towards the Colonel. Stanhope appreciates that it is really Osborne who holds the Company together, not himself, because he has come to rely so heavily on Osborne as the war has progressed. Nothing has really been gained by these deaths and Sherriff uses Osborne's death in particular to reinforce the idea of this war's destruction of the best men of his generation.

Throughout the play, however, Sherriff also shows that death is not the only means of wasting a life: Stanhope has virtually suffered a nervous breakdown, changing from the self-assured, sportsman and hero of Raleigh's description, to a confused and moody wreck, who doubts his own abilities and constantly looks to Osborne for reassurance. Raleigh, on the other hand, loses his innocence: he learns a difficult lesson as he comes to realise that Stanhope is not the man he once knew and that the war has changed his friend forever. Ultimately Raleigh also loses his life - within a few minutes of his first experience of battle - but not before he has witnessed the physical and emotional damage that the war can bring about. Had either Stanhope or Raleigh lived, it is unlikely that they would ever have fully recovered from their experiences. Stanhope actually realises this already, as he shows in his conversation with Osborne, when he says that if he survives he will go away by himself for a long time, to recover his health, before trying to face Madge again.

Another example of futility comes in a seemingly strange conversation when Osborne and Stanhope discuss the fate of worms. The two men agree that worms probably have no idea in which direction they are travelling and how rotten and confusing this must be for them. This minor conversation could be interpreted as a reference to the equal pointlessness of the men's existence - they also have very little idea of where they are going, or why, and yet as Osborne says - with more than an air of sarcasm, this pointlessness and confusion is dreaded by the worms more than anything else. He is implying that there are worse situations to be in than wasting your time drifting aimlessly; being killed, without ever really understanding the reason, for example, could as easily befall the worm or the soldier.

The choice of *Alice's Adventures in Wonderland* as reading material for Osborne is also interesting. Osborne quotes from the book to Trotter, who finds the passage pointless and playfully mocks Osborne for reading a children's book. Of course, Osborne's point is that it *is* pointless - not just the passage quoted, but everything - this story represents how little meaning there is in the men's lives, and how nonsensical the whole war has become. For most of the men, especially those like Stanhope and Raleigh, the point of joining up was for the "adventure" and to do their duty, not to sit around in trenches, waiting to be blown up, or being sent on pointless raids into No Man's Land.

As the play progresses, these themes become more noticeable and more intense, marked by the deaths of the likeable and innocent in the forms of first Osborne and then Raleigh. The attack which has always been anticipated throughout the play seems to serve no purpose, shown by Stanhope's suggestion to the Sergeant-Major that they must hold their ground no matter what the other Companies around them might do. This implies that he doesn't intend the German army to progress at all, showing that there is no hope for any meaningful breakthrough for either side. Sherriff, it would seem, wanted to portray the war as a pointless exercise, achieving nothing and costing more than it was worth.

BOREDOM AND TENSION

Most of the play is spent waiting for something to happen, whether it is a raid, the impending attack or the serving of a meal. Hardy tells us right at the beginning of the play that the men can sit in boredom for hours and hours and then, suddenly, without warning, something unexpected will happen.

The tension created by this sense of anticipation provokes different responses in each of the characters. Hibbert, for example, dreads going up into the trenches and longs for the waiting to continue - anything as long as he doesn't have to face the realities of his situation. He spends most of his time asleep in his dugout, not mixing with the other men. By avoiding them he also avoids the issue of what might be about to happen, because he is not there to hear it being discussed. His supposed illness is his means of trying to escape, although it also tells us a lot about his personality. Hibbert's reaction is a form of denial: by pretending to be unwell and avoiding the others, he is trying to appear as though the war has not really affected him psychologically, but that it has made him physically ill. The truth, of course, is revealed during his argument with Stanhope, when he is forced to confess his real feelings.

Stanhope on the other hand, 'copes' by keeping busy, not sleeping and drinking himself into oblivion. By doing this he not only takes his mind off the reality of his life, but also helps to pass the time doing anything other than thinking - a necessity of his position which has become abhorrent to him. In addition to not thinking about his current situation any more than is absolutely necessary, Stanhope also seems to have been avoiding thoughts of his past. Raleigh's arrival necessities a resurgence of these memories and, for the first time, he tells Osborne about his feelings for Madge. Osborne is Stanhope's closest friend and yet he has never spoken of Raleigh's sister before. He has obviously found it necessary to block out his memories of the past, in order to maintain a semblance of a focus on the present. Remembering these things only seems to add to his tensions which become more obvious as the raid approaches. He paces the floor, glances about anxiously, checks his watch repeatedly - showing that the strain of waiting is making him even more nervous than normal. He also busies himself with the last-minute preparations so as to avoid thinking about what might happen.

Osborne tries to help wherever he can and relieves his boredom by reading *Alice's Adventures in Wonderland*. He is a great observer of everything which is going on around him. He talks to the others, helping to relieve their nerves, especially Raleigh, who has no idea what to expect. Probably the most tense moment in the play is the scene between Raleigh and Osborne immediately prior to the raid. Once they have finalised their plans, Osborne suggests that they try to forget about the raid for the final few minutes before it commences. It takes several attempts and a quotation from *Alice in Wonderland* before Osborne succeeds in changing the subject. The tension actually seems to increase as they discuss their homes and talk of Osborne visiting Raleigh after the war. There is an unspoken fear that, in all probability, one or other of these men may not return and they make plans for the future to cover this up.

Trotter eats, thinks about eating, or talks about eating, and writes to his wife of mundane, everyday matters, such as his garden and the lice which have infested his clothing. He has created a chart of circles to count down the hours until they can be relieved and go back down the line. Trotter uses humour to overcome these difficult situations, although there is always the underlying hint that he feels much more than he expresses.

Only Raleigh, the new recruit is, as yet, unaffected by the boredom, as he is keen to impress the others, so he pays attention and makes sure that he is doing his duty to the best of his ability. Although he is unaware of what lies ahead in the raid, the tension of waiting to go out into No Man's Land is obvious and his nerves start to get the better of his excitement, although Osborne helps to calm him down. Once Osborne has been killed, Raleigh's sense of adventure and excited anticipation disappear, to be replaced by the same sense of sorrow and foreboding as the rest of the men.

In reality these feelings of boredom and tension were common among serving soldiers in the First World War. Their feelings of terror during battles could be said to have been increased by the fact that so much of their time was spent doing mundane and repetitive tasks, waiting for something to happen. It was all or nothing.

Sherriff's portrayal of these aspects, therefore, adds an air of realism to the play which the early audiences, some of whom would have been former soldiers, would have recognised. He wanted the audience to understand his perspective that the war hadn't worn men down due to the fighting, but due to so many other factors, of which boredom and tension were just two. As the play progresses, he therefore diminishes the amount of boredom and increases the levels of tension, to show that there was an element of ebb and flow to what happened, but that, essentially, it remained the same vicious circle, ultimately leading nowhere.

SCHOOLDAYS AND HEROES

There is a strong comparison drawn between life in the trenches and at a "public" school. Not only were Raleigh and Stanhope at the same school, but Osborne, in private life, was a school master. At the time of the First World War, the title "public" school was given to fee-paying establishments, of which many were also boarding schools. Therefore, there is an atmosphere of the school dormitory in the dugout, and a definite sense of hierarchy, with certain officers taking precedence over others, and the emphasis being on experience and seniority. For instance, right at the beginning of the play, Hardy points out the best bed in the dugout to Osborne, telling him that the others do not have bottoms to them. As the senior officer of his Company, Hardy has the best bed, while the other officers have to make do with whatever is left. Stanhope, on the other hand, designates the best bed to Osborne, preferring to sleep nearer to the table, so he can work during the night without disturbing anyone else.

Stanhope is given the air of the "head boy", looking after those younger or less experienced than himself, especially the new boy - Raleigh. Although we are led to believe that Stanhope was happy to wear this mantle while at school, it does not sit well with him now. He says that he used to enjoy looking after Raleigh and the influence that he was able to exert over the younger boy, but now he feels uncomfortable at having so much additional responsibility thrust upon him. He also wishes that he could have been spared the indignity of having Raleigh witness what has become of him - he feels that his hero's crown has slipped and does not want to crush Raleigh's image of him. It would seem that Stanhope took his status at school quite seriously. Raleigh recalls Stanhope's attitude towards smoking and drinking when they were at school, which goes to show how much of an impact the war has had, being as Stanhope now drinks so much himself.

Raleigh, on the other hand, is the new boy is eager to please and do well, just as he probably would have been at school. His personality makes him keen to learn, although he is as yet unsure of the rules and protocols which exist in the trenches. At school, Raleigh had worshipped Stanhope and looked up to him as someone worthy of respect, finding it impossible to see a fault in Stanhope's personality. He is keen that this relationship should continue in the trenches and hopes that Stanhope will not object to his presence. Osborne has to try and warn Raleigh about his hero's altered personality and the effect that the war has had on him. Raleigh's hopes for a resumption of his friendship with Stanhope may be because he assumes that the continuation of certain aspects of his life at home will give him an increased sense of security - reminding him, perhaps, of happier days at school.

Osborne, with his worldly experience is the voice of reason and sanity - the housemaster. He offers sensible advice and provides a caring, responsible figure for the others to turn to. As a former school-master, he is perfectly suited to this role as he understands the problems of boys who find themselves away from home. It must be remembered that Stanhope, when he first went out to the front, and Raleigh, when he arrives, are extremely young - and have arrived straight from school. Osborne's presence must be very welcome and reassuring to both of them. A good example of this relationship is when Stanhope asks Osborne to tuck him up in bed - this shows not only Stanhope's youth, but also Osborne's caring and understanding nature.

We also have Mason, who in the role of servant, helps recreate the public school hierarchy. The officers chastise him for not bringing any pepper to go with their soup, and he worries (quite disproportionately) about the prospect of having to serve apricots instead of the desired pineapple. His worries serve to remind us of his 'inferior' status, when compared to the officers.

Trotter is the only one of the officers who, it would seem, did not attend a public school. This is demonstrated by his tone and language, which is more colloquial than the others. Also, we learn that he has risen from the ranks, which would have been the only course open to him at the beginning of the war. This is interesting, as it means that rather than being commissioned as an officer from the very beginning, he has worked his way up, by being good at what he does. The difference in his education could provide a reason why Trotter keeps his views to himself most of the time: although they are all friendly enough, he possibly does not feel that he really fits in with the others.

Stanhope's treatment of Hibbert, when the latter tries to evade his duties, is reminiscent of schooldays. Although he is obviously more extreme in his language and the nature of his threats, one can easily imagine Stanhope berating Hibbert for refusing to turn out for a rugby match, or not doing his best in the last game of cricket. Hibbert is, in fact, the only member of the company who does not show Stanhope very much respect, but then we are not told what his background is, so we do not know whether he is a public schoolboy. His language ties in with most of the other officers, but his behaviour is not so honourable as theirs. His role in the play demonstrates a less appealing type of personality whose position at school would probably have been the boy who cheated in his exams.

Sherriff employs many references to rugby and cricket which help reinforce this "public schoolboy" image of England as it was before the First World War and most of the men attempt to maintain these old school standards throughout: by respecting their superiors, not questioning their orders and being loyal to one another.

This portrayal would have been easily recognisable to many people in the audience of the early productions, some of whom would have attended public schools themselves. Even if they hadn't however, they would have been able to see similarities between the characters portrayed and the men with whom they had served. The hero-worship element is also not a surprising portrayal as it was a common aspect of both public schools and the First World War.

In developing these two themes, Sherriff shows how they could easily break down under the pressure and tension of the front lines and how this made that environment so different from the much easier schooldays. The fact that Stanhope eventually regains his heroic status shows us that all is not really lost, but the journey through which he and Raleigh travel helps the audience to realise how great the cost was to their generation, in terms of losing the familiar aspects of their lives.

THE EFFECTS OF WAR ON THE INDIVIDUAL

This is a common theme within the literature of the First World War and it is not surprising that it features in *Journey's End*, bearing in mind Sherriff's first-hand experiences of the conflict. As well as undergoing some changes himself, he would also have witnessed the ways in which the war affected everyone around him.

As a play, rather than a novel, *Journey's End* provides a different opportunity for examining the concept of how war might affect an individual. Rather than relying on language and literary devices, Sherriff had the advantage of being able to use expression and physical actions to portray this element. In this way, for example, Stanhope's dependence on alcohol is more poignant because the actor can portray, with a look at the bottle or a pause over the glass, how much he needs that next drink. Equally, the deaths of Osborne and Raleigh are not only brought more vividly to life, but so is Stanhope's reaction, in that the audience can see his grief on his face and hear it in his voice.

The most obvious character who Sherriff wants the audience to see as being changed by his war experiences, is Stanhope and this is made clear from his very first appearance. The audience has already been made aware by Raleigh that he and Stanhope attended school together and we have also been told that Raleigh is a 'well-built, healthy-looking boy of about eighteen, with the new uniform of a second lieutenant.' A little later, when Stanhope enters the dugout, his description is a little different, but in quite subtle ways. We are informed at once that he is 'no more than a boy' and that he takes care of his appearance, making him seem, at first glance, quite similar to Raleigh. Then, however, Sherriff points out his 'old and war-stained' uniform and the 'pallor under his skin' which, coupled with the 'dark shadows under his eyes' give away the length of time he has spent in the trenches and his exhaustion. The difference between the two men, as well as their similarities in age, helps the audience to immediately see the impact that being in the trenches has had on Stanhope.

This aspect is reinforced by Raleigh's descriptions of his time at school with Stanhope, which can then be contrasted with Stanhope's actual behaviour within the play, which the audience can witness at first hand. This is probably most obvious in the scene centred around Raleigh's letter. The disparity between the actual content of Raleigh's letter and Stanhope's violent reaction to him is so marked that it leaves the audience in no doubt as to Stanhope's state of mind. This, coupled with Raleigh's response to Stanhope at the time, which borders on fear, allows us to really see the changes in him through the eyes, not only of someone who really knows him, but also of someone who is still an innocent.

Stanhope is the most obviously war-weary character in the play. He has the shortest temper and is prone to flaring up at the slighted provocation, partly because he is always tired or drunk and partly because the responsibility for all the men around him has fallen on his shoulders. We learn that taking responsibility for others is not a new concept for Stanhope, but during war, those responsibilities are significantly heightened. They no longer relate to school or sports activities, but to life and death. This has clearly come to weigh heavily on Stanhope as time has progressed.

In order to see how the war impacts on Stanhope, we can also look at how it affects his old friend Raleigh and how their relationship changes. At the beginning of the play, Raleigh shows a keen innocence for what lies ahead. The audience is aware of his naiveté because of the conversation that has taken place between Osborne and Hardy, which has revealed a little about Stanhope and something of the realities of the war. Raleigh retains this innocence until after the incident regarding his letter, at which point he becomes a little more guarded around Stanhope, although he is still excited when he is chosen to accompany Osborne on the raid. It is only after Osborne's death that we can really perceive any change in Raleigh and that is brought about by Stanhope's altered attitude to him. Raleigh is confused by Stanhope's reaction to the loss of Osborne, interpreting the dinner as a celebration, rather than a means of forgetting. Again, this really shows the inexperience of Raleigh and it angers Stanhope that his friend has failed to comprehend the situation. The realisation of how much Stanhope cared for Osborne hits Raleigh quite hard, mainly because he doesn't know how to react anymore. His friendship with Stanhope has altered and there is too much distance between them now for him to cross back.

Although the war has an enormous impact on Stanhope's character, it is fair to say that the greatest alterations which the audience witnesses are caused by death, rather than the actual conflict. Firstly, following Osborne's death, Stanhope is initially humorous and hearty, trying to hide from the pain of his loss. Then he turns his anger and grief onto Raleigh, who probably respects him more than anyone else. Finally, when Raleigh dies, the audience sees a true transformation in a character, as Stanhope cares, with a remarkable intensity and compassion, for his dying friend. In this way, Sherriff gives his audience hope, showing us that, no matter how bad the damage, the man himself always had a chance of redemption and was never completely lost.

FAMILY

Whilst these men are all very different, in terms of background, experience and personality, they have become like a family and have adopted roles within that family. There is a powerful sense of belonging and of loyalty which most of the men exhibit throughout the play and those who do not are chastised for their attitude.

Osborne, the oldest and wisest, is nicknamed "Uncle" - a well deserved and appropriate epithet since he is always on hand with sensible advice, is supremely loyal and kind, yet not overbearing or interfering. His maturity and experience, both before and during the war, help him to understand the others. Osborne's adoption of this nickname enhances this family theme and encourages the audience or reader to look for further examples of it.

Stanhope, despite his youth, is a father-figure to his men - which was not an uncommon role for company commanders in the First World War. He has to take all the tough decisions and deal with the consequences both of his own and others' actions. This responsibility weighs heavily on one so young, and has taken its toll on Stanhope, who is on the verge of a nervous breakdown relying heavily on the senior members of his "family" for support. Their loyalty and respect for him are obvious - and well deserved. Despite his many faults, he always puts them first.

Raleigh is the equivalent of the youngest son in the family - looking to his elders for advice and approval. He worships Stanhope blindly and his attachment to his friend is clear: when writing to his family at home, he makes no mention of Stanhope's problems with alcohol or his changed temperament - putting any noticeable changes in Stanhope's personality down to tiredness and overwork. Like many younger sons, he doesn't yet have a fixed idea of what his future holds and is content, for the time being, at least, to follow in the footsteps of those who have preceded him.

The role of older brother goes to Trotter, who is quiet, considerate and has a good sense of humour which sees the family through difficult times. He keeps his own counsel and doesn't interfere but is willing to help when asked. Again, he is loyal to Stanhope, but in a less obvious, more considered manner. He is not blind to Stanhope's faults, but understands their cause and his age and experience allow him to be more tolerant of his surroundings and of the behaviour of others.

Hibbert is the "Black Sheep" of the family, and he sometimes embarrasses those around him by his comments and outbursts. He is the only selfish member of the "family", and his loyalties lie entirely with himself. He shows little or no respect for Stanhope or his fellow officers and his main concern is how to avoid any further involvement in the war.

Mason, in his role as cook, is the equivalent of the household servant, tending to the needs of the family. His loyalty is to all of them, but he answers mainly to Stanhope, who is perceived as the head of the house.

Sherriff's portrayal of this family setup creates a homely and comforting atmosphere which contrasts at once with the threat of the attack and the tension that is created in anticipating it. This reminds the audience that, for the soldiers at the front, the thoughts of home and family would often provide solace at difficult times, helping them to cope with their fears and troubles. Sherriff takes the family element to a higher pitch after Osborne's death, allowing the audience to see the depth of Stanhope's loss and how this event will impact on everyone involved, just as it would in civilian life, if the men had actually been related to each other.

HUMOUR

There is a very effective use of humour, usually of a 'gallows' style, throughout the play.

Very early on, during Hardy's conversation with Osborne, the use of humour demonstrates the need for relief from the everyday horrors of war. The number of rats, the condition of the dugout and beds, the poor storage of ammunition, all of which are very important, are treated in a flippant, lighthearted manner. Other matters, too are treated in the same way, for example the lack of pepper to go with the officer's soup brings a wry comment from Trotter, whose interest in food provides the source of several other jokes. The fact that important and insignificant issues are treated in the same manner shows that, even things which in peacetime might seem unimportant, can, at times of extreme stress, take on a completely different emphasis.

This use of humour actually helps define the surroundings and the men's state of mind. This could probably have been achieved without the humour, but it would have been less effective, especially when one remembers that *Journey's End* is a play and is, therefore, meant to be seen as a performance. The setting of the dugout and the building tension needs some form of relief, otherwise the audience would find it too oppressive. The realistic use of humour makes the whole situation more human, which in turn draws the audience into the world of these men.

Sherriff's use of humour is, at times, more subtle - for example near the end of the play, just before the attack, when Trotter is singing in his dugout, Stanhope throws him a few coins, as though he were a street performer, and Trotter replies in kind. This humour helps in the creation of the atmosphere of camaraderie which is what has kept the men going in the dugout. This is reflected in many of the memoirs written by soldiers who served during the First World War. Without being able to crack a joke, or have a laugh, the tension would have been almost unbearable.

TRIVIA AND REVIEWS

There are quite a few extra bits of information which don't really fit into any of the foregoing chapters, some of which are included here more for fun anything else. However, they do help to provide some insight into what Sherriff might have been thinking when he was righting and overseeing the production of Journey's End.

TRIVIA:

According to early productions, the pronunciation of some of the characters is different to how we might imagine. It should be born in mind that, in those days, the actors would have used 'received' pronunciation, with only Mason and Trotter having a lower class background, which is reflected in their speech:

• Stanhope was pronounced "Stan'up";

• Raleigh was pronounced "Raw-ley";

• Osborne was pronounced "Oz-b'n".

Having starred in the first two performances of Journey's End at the Apollo Theatre, the young Laurence Olivier was unable to continue with the remaining cast when the play was transferred to the Savoy Theatre. Years later, Olivier stated that his favourite theatre role had been playing Stanhope in Journey's End. Given the roles that Olivier must have performed, and that he only played the part for two shows, this is high praise indeed.

REVIEWS:

When *Journey's End* was first performed at the Apollo Theatre on the 9th and 10th of December 1928, the critics arrived to watch the production on the second showing and Sherriff waited anxiously on the morning of the 11th to discover their opinion. He need not have feared: the play was well received.

Hannan Swaffer - a much feared critic, writing for the Daily Express, began his piece with the headline: "The greatest of all war plays", continuing:

"A new dramatist, R. C. Sherriff, achieved the distinction of compelling to real emotion an audience who were watching a play almost without plot, with no women in the cast!... It was a remarkable achievement... *Journey's End* is perhaps the greatest of all war plays... This is the English theatre at its best... There is no shirking the facts: no concession to fashion... It is perfectly acted; each actor cuts a little cameo of stark reality... All London should flock to see it. It carries a great lesson - one that is nobly told..."

Later that evening, James Agate, critic for The Times gave his weekly theatre review on the radio. In this he usually spoke of three or four productions, but on that evening he dedicated his entire programme to *Journey's End*, saying:

"I've just seen a play called *Journey's End*, and I shall talk of nothing else tonight but of this fine piece of work. I have never been so deeply moved, so enthralled, so exalted... Lest you think it a sombre unrelieved tragedy I must tell you of a cook-batman whose every appearance brought the house down."

After the production went on at The Savoy Theatre on 21st January 1929, Sherriff again wondered whether the critics would be kind and, again, his fears were unfounded. The headlines spoke for themselves:

"This noble war play" - the Morning Post

"Great War Drama" - the Daily Mail

"Fine New War Play" - the Mirror

"No one should miss seeing this play" - the Daily News

The reviews themselves were even more fulsome:

"Everyone must see *Journey's End*... It could and should be translated into the language of every ex-ally and ex-enemy" said the critic in the Chronicle.

"Once inside the theatre, no one will be other than enthralled," was the comment in the Daily Sketch.

"Mr R. C. Sherriff's war play *Journey's End*, made a profound impression when it was given a trial production by the Stage Society in December, and now that it has been put on for a run at the Savoy Theatre we may look to it to make an impression equally profound upon a wider public... The author has achieved that rare feat of bringing to complete accomplishment what he set out to do... not for a long time has any serious play been so rapturously received." is how the play was reported in the Telegraph.

Sherriff himself put the success of the play down to its realism: he hadn't set out to preach a message about war and its rights or wrongs, but to portray it as it really was. This allowed former soldiers, war widows and anyone who had any understanding of the conflict to relate to and learn from it.

EXAMINATION/CONTROLLED ASSESSMENT ADVICE

The intention of this section of the study guide is to encourage students to look more thoroughly into a given theme, topic or character and then learn to apply this method to other studies.

Examination Question

OCR - Unit A662 Modern Drama
1. Text-based Questions
Example:
Look at the speech between Raleigh and Osborne at the beginning of the play, starting:
Osborne: My name's Osborne. I'm second in command...
and ending:
Osborne: If you notice a - difference in Stanhope...

Question:
How does Sherriff make this such an important conversation in the play? Remember to support you ideas with details from the passage and the rest of the play.

- The textual question will always take this form, although the content and nature of the question will obviously vary.
- Examiners are looking for students to not just look at the effect of the speech given at the time, but also how it impacts throughout the play.
- In this instance, the immediate importance of this conversation is that it gives the audience the background information on the relationship between Raleigh and Stanhope, as well as informing us of some of Stanhope's characteristics and his friendship with Raleigh's sister.

- We also learn a little about Raleigh: his diffidence and hero worship being his foremost characteristics at this point. We discover the extent of Osborne's loyalty to Stanhope, as he tries to protect him from Raleigh's idealism.
- Within the wider context of the rest of the play, the audience will later remember Raleigh's tone of affection and admiration, especially when Stanhope reacts so violently over Raleigh's letter. Also Osborne's calmness in the letter scene harks back to this conversation, as he has already realised that Raleigh loves Stanhope too much to do him any harm.

In answering a question like this, students need to show that they have understood the characters involved, and can interpret their actions, using relevant quotes from the text where necessary to back up these opinions.

2. Character-based Questions
Example:
Explore the importance of Hibbert's character in the play.
Remember to support your ideas with details from the play.

- This second question is nearly always character-based, but may also include a specific theme, scene or relationship from the play as well.
- The examiners are asking students to refer to the play widely, so they should not only address the character/theme/relationship in question, but also examine how that impacts on the play and other characters.
- This question is looking for an opinion and may require the student to take a stance, either positively or negatively about a character and their portrayal in the play.
- In the example given above, students could discuss how and why Sherriff has used such a negative character, showing his impact, especially on Stanhope and exploring the reasons why Hibbert's inclusion helps Sherriff to develop the other characters.

Controlled Assessment

Edexcel English Literature Unit 3 - Contemporary Drama Task

Students are required to examine and answer a question based around the development within the play of one of the following:

1. A single character;
2. A single theme;
3. A relationship between to characters.

Character Question:
Explore the ways in which a central character is developed in the drama.

- In the case of *Journey's End*, the term 'central character' can only really be applied to Stanhope, Osborne and Raleigh.
- In all three instances, students must remember the question relates to the development of these characters, not merely to the portrayal and journeys that they take through the course of the play.
- If examining Stanhope, for example, students can look at his personality from Raleigh's point of view, giving a pre-war perspective of his younger days, then show how Hardy sees him, then look at Hibbert's and Osborne's differing views and finally the ways in which Stanhope deals with Osborne's and Raleigh's deaths. Effectively, it can be shown that Stanhope comes full circle in his journey, returning to his heroic status in Raleigh's eyes.
- Similar principles can be applied to other characters, looking at what Sherriff tells us of their background, how others react to them and how they behave towards their fellow officers. This helps to show how the characters develop. Osborne is probably the hardest character to demonstrate within this question, despite his importance to the play, because of his death in the raid.

Theme Question:
Explore the ways in which a central theme is developed in the drama.

- In this case, the term 'central theme' could be applied to subjects like Futility, Boredom, Hero-worship or Humour.
- In examining these themes, students are required to show how they are developed throughout the play, so they must focus on giving evidence from several areas.

- For example, if looking at hero-worship, students could explore how Raleigh initially describes his schoolboy relationship with Stanhope, then demonstrate how this begins to break down during the episode over the letter and finally examine how Stanhope's status is restored at the end.

Relationship Question:
Explore the ways in which a relationship between two central characters is developed in this drama.

- Here there are really two main relationships on which to focus: the one between Stanhope and Osborne, or the one between Stanhope and Raleigh.
- The relationship between Stanhope and Osborne is more important to the plot, but the relationship between Stanhope and Raleigh probably gives students more scope for exploring the development aspect of the question.
- If choosing the relationship between Stanhope and Osborne, students could examine the conversation between Hardy and Osborne, showing very early on in the play how Osborne 'loves' and respects Stanhope. Then they could move on to Stanhope and Osborne's conversation about Raleigh, which demonstrates Stanhope's dependence on Osborne and Osborne's ability to offer sound advice. Their parting shows the depth of feeling on both sides and Stanhope's grief when Osborne is killed is clearly shocking to Raleigh, enabling the audience to grasp his loss.
- The relationship question must be addressed from both sides, looking at the situation from the perspective of both characters.

GENERAL ADVICE TO STUDENTS

Although examinations can seem daunting, especially when the topic is as wide as First World War Literature, it is worth remembering the following simple tips:

- **Be prepared.** Read as much as possible beforehand; make sure you have revised well enough.

- **Read the question.** In other words, read it carefully, several times if necessary to be sure that you have a full understanding of what is expected. It is a very simple mistake to think you have understood the requirements only to find that you have completely misinterpreted them. Think about key words. What is the question actually asking of you?

- **Answer the question.** Another common error is to get stuck in a train of thought and forget that what you are writing might not actually be answering the question in hand. You should stick to the topic required, even though you might have thought of a brilliant piece of analysis - if it doesn't relate to the question, it doesn't belong in your answer.

- **Allow enough time.** The examination paper will give you a guide as to how long to allow for each question. Think about the fact that you must plan your essay, deciding in advance how you want to approach the topic in hand. Don't forget to allow a few minutes at the end, just to check over what you have written.

- Extra marks will be awarded for **spelling, punctuation and grammar**, so it is worth paying attention to these aspects.

- **Use quotations wisely.** Most importantly, ensure that you quote accurately. You have the text in front of you, so there is no excuse for errors. Try to incorporate quotes within your own sentences. For example:

You could say -

Sherriff tells us that Trotter is overweight as his 'tunic appears to be on the verge of bursting at the waist'.

However, it would be more sophisticated to say -

Trotter's 'red, fat and round' face and his tunic, which 'appears to be on the verge of bursting at the waist' leave us in no doubt that he is keen on his food.

Good luck!

FURTHER READING

To the Last Man: Spring 1918
by Lyn MacDonald

As with all of Lyn MacDonald's excellent books, To the Last Man tells its story through the words of the people who were there. It is not restricted to a British perspective, but tells of the first few months of 1918 and their momentous consequences from every angle. The author gives just the right amount of background information of a political and historical nature to keep the reader interested and informed, while leaving the centre-stage to those who really matter... the men themselves. This is an invaluable book for anyone studying Journey's End as it helps, probably more than any other book, in the understanding of the personalities involved and the time through which they were living.

Strange Meeting
by Susan Hill

Strange Meeting is a beautiful and moving book. It is the story of two young men, who meet in the worst circumstances, yet manage to overcome their surroundings and form a deep and lasting friendship. Susan Hill writes so evocatively that the reader is automatically drawn into the lives of these men: the sights, sounds and even smells which they witness are brought to life. It is a book about war and its effects; it is also a story of love, both conventional and 'forbidden'; of human relationships of every variety. This is a tale told during the worst of times, about the best of men.

Not About Heroes

by Stephen MacDonald

Probably one of the most underrated First World War plays, this details the meeting between Wilfred Owen and Siegfried Sassoon. It is a humourous, tragic and above all, moving account of this friendship and is based on diary entries and extracts from autobiographies.

The Complete Memoirs of George Sherston

by Siegfried Sassoon

An autobiographical account of Sassoon's life before and during the First World War. Sassoon has changed the names of the characters and George Sherston (Sassoon) is not a poet. This trilogy (made up of Memoirs of a Fox Hunting Man, Memoirs of an Infantry Officer and Sherston's Progress) demonstrates the effects of the war on both the serving soldiers and those left at home.

For a list of the fictional characters and their factual counterparts, see Appendix II of **Siegfried Sassoon** *by John Stuart Roberts*.

The Return of the Soldier

by Rebecca West

Written in 1918, this home-front novel gives a useful insight into the trauma of war, as seen through the eyes of three women. Chris Baldry, an officer and husband of Kitty, returns home suffering from shell-shock and amnesia, believing that he is still in a relationship with Margaret Allington - his first love. Kitty, Margaret and Chris's cousin, Jenny, must decide whether to leave Chris in his make-believe world, safe from the war; or whether to 'cure' him and risk his future welfare once he returns to being a soldier.

All Quiet on the Western Front

by Erich Maria Remarque

Written from first-hand experience of life in the trenches, this novel is the moving account of the lives of a group of young German soldiers during the First World War. The fact that this, often shocking, story is told from a German perspective demonstrates the universal horrors of the war and the sympathy between men of both sides for others enduring the same hardships as themselves.

In addition, students of *Journey's End* could also watch *Blackadder Goes Forth* starring Rowan Atkinson paying particular attention to the final episode. Although this screenplay was written in the late 20th century, much of the atmosphere and 'gallows' humour could prove useful in understanding this play, especially when students are unable to see a live performance.

BIBLIOGRAPHY

The First World War
by John Keegan

Chronology of the Great War, 1914-1918
Edited by Lord Edward Gleichen

To the Last Man: Spring 1918
by Lyn MacDonald

Rosebriars Trust
rosebriars.org.uk

Journey's End
by R C Sherriff

Strange Meeting
by Susan Hill

The Return of the Soldier
by Rebecca West

All Quiet on the Western Front
by Erich Maria Remarque

Scars Upon My Heart
Edited by Catherine Reilly

Never Such Innocence
Edited by Martin Stephen

The British Expeditionary Force 1914-15
Bruce Gudmundsson

No Leading Lady: An Autobiography
by R C Sherriff

The Private War Letters of R C Sherriff

OTHER TITLES

GREAT WAR LITERATURE STUDY GUIDE E-BOOKS:

NOVELS & PLAYS

All Quiet on the Western Front
Birdsong
Journey's End (A-Level or GCSE)
Regeneration
The Eye in the Door
The Ghost Road
A Long Long Way
The First Casualty
Strange Meeting
The Return of the Soldier
The Accrington Pals
Not About Heroes
Oh What a Lovely War

POET BIOGRAPHIES AND POETRY ANALYSIS:

Herbert Asquith
Harold Begbie
John Peale Bishop
Edmund Blunden
Vera Brittain
Rupert Brooke
Thomas Burke
May Wedderburn Cannan
Margaret Postgate Cole
Alice Corbin
E E Cummings

Nancy Cunard
T S Eliot
Eleanor Farjeon
Gilbert Frankau
Robert Frost
Wilfrid Wilson Gibson
Anna Gordon Keown
Robert Graves
Julian Grenfell
Ivor Gurney
Thomas Hardy
Alan P Herbert
Agnes Grozier Herbertson
W N Hodgson
A E Housman
Geoffrey Anketell Studdert Kennedy
Winifred M Letts
Amy Lowell
E A Mackintosh
John McCrae
Charlotte Mew
Edna St Vincent Millay
Ruth Comfort Mitchell
Harriet Monroe
Edith Nesbit
Robert Nichols
Wilfred Owen
Jessie Pope
Ezra Pound
Florence Ripley Mastin
Isaac Rosenberg
Carl Sandburg
Siegfried Sassoon
Alan Seeger
Charles Hamilton Sorley
Wallace Stevens
Sara Teasdale
Edward Wyndham Tennant
Lesbia Thanet
Edward Thomas

Iris Tree
Katharine Tynan Hinkson
Robert Ernest Vernède
Arthur Graeme West

Please note that e-books are only available direct from our Web site at www.greatwarliterature.co.uk and cannot be purchased through bookshops.

NOTES

Printed in Great Britain
by Amazon

80501923R00056